Y0-BZG-511

Ernest Hemingway:

The Sun Also Rises and Other Works

wouldn't be any good. I'll go if you like. But I Br

Writers and Their Works

Ernest Hemingway:

The Sun Also Rises and Other Works

Kevin Alexander Boon

Marshall Cavendish
Benchmark
New York

This book is gratefully dedicated to my mentor and friend, Louise Hawes, for her kind words, gentle spirit, and unwavering encouragement.

With thanks to Forrest Robinson, professor of American Studies and Literature, University of California, Santa Cruz, for his expert review of this manuscript

Marshall Cavendish Benchmark
99 White Plains Road
Tarrytown, NY 10591
www.marshallcavendish.us

Library of Congress Cataloging-in-Publication Data

Boon, Kevin A.
Ernest Hemingway : the sun always rises and other works / by Kevin Alexander Boon.
p. cm. — (Writers and their works)
Summary: "A biography of writer Ernest Hemingway that describes his era, his major works—especially The Sun Also Rises and The Old Man and the Sea—his life, and the legacy of his writing"—Provided by publisher.
Includes bibliographical references and index.
ISBN-13: 978-0-7614-2590-8
1. Hemingway, Ernest, 1899–1961. 2. Authors, American—20th century—Biography. I. Title. II. Series.
PS3515.E37Z58253 2007
813'.52—dc22

All quotations are cited in the text. Notes containing additional information and sources are included in the Notes section.

Photo research by Linda Sykes Picture Research, Hilton Head, SC

The photographs in this book are used by permission and through the courtesy of: The Granger Collection: cover, 14, 20, 34, 44; Ernest Hemingway Collection/John F. Kennedy Presidential Library, Boston, MA: 8. 11. 16. 22; Hulton Archive/Getty Images: 27, 36; Cornell Capa Photos by Robert Capa ©2001/Magnum Photos: 42; Getty Images: 46, 111; Photofest: 54. 106; The Everett Collection: 81; Princeton University Library: 94, 104; ©Twentieth Century Fox Film Corp. All Rights Reserved/ The Everett Collection: 123.

Publisher: Michelle Bisson
Art Director: Anahid Hamparian
Designer: Sonia Chaghatzbanian

Printed in China
1 3 5 6 4 2

Contents

ouldn't be any good. I'll go if you like. But I   Bre
n't live quietly in the country. Not with my own true lo
ow."
it rotten? There isn't any use my telling you I love yo
know I love you."
not talk. Talking's all bilge. I'm going away from you,
Michael's coming back."
are you going away?"
er for you. Better for me." The Sun Also Rises "Couldn't w
n the country for a while?"   Jake said.
ouldn't be any good. I'll go if you like. But I   Bre
n't live quietly in the country. Not with my own true lo
ow."
it rotten? There isn't any use my telling you I love yo
know I love you."
not talk. Talking's all bilge. I'm going away from you,
Michael's coming back."
are you going away?"
er for you. Better for me." *The Sun Also Rises* "Couldn't w
n the country for a while?"   Jake said.
ouldn't be any good. I'll go if you like. But I   Bre
n't live quietly in the country. Not with my own true lo
ow."
it rotten? There isn't any use my telling you I love yo
know I love you."
not talk. Talking's all bilge. I'm going away from you,
Michael's coming back."
are you going away?"
er for you. Better for me." *The Sun Also Rises*
ldn't we go off in the country for a while?"   Jake said.
ouldn't be any good. I'll go if you like. But I   Bre
n't live quietly in the country. Not with my own true lo
ow."
it rotten? There isn't any use my telling you I love yo
know I love you."
not talk. Talking's all bilge. I'm going away from you,
Michael's coming back."
are you going away?"
er for you. Better for me." *The Sun Also Rises*
ldn't we go off in the country for a while?"   Jake said.
ouldn't be any good. I'll go if you like. But I   Bre
n't live quietly in the country. Not with my own true lo
ow."

Part I:
The Life of Ernest Hemingway

As a writer, Ernest Hemingway had a reputation for machismo.
As an infant, his mother outfitted him in dresses.

Chapter 1

The Man They Called "Papa"

Childhood

Ernest Miller Hemingway was born at 8:00 AM on July 21, 1899, in Oak Park, Illinois, a suburb of Chicago. Hemingway's father, Clarence Edmonds "Ed" Hemingway, was a devoutly religious physician. He introduced Ernest to the outdoors when the boy was barely seven weeks old by taking him to the family cottage on Walloon Lake. Ed Hemingway, a tall, strong, bearded man, taught Ernest to hunt and fish and to share his love of the outdoors. Ernest's mother, Grace Hall Hemingway, was a talented singer who debuted at New York's Madison Square Garden, but, after her marriage to Ed, fulfilled her gift by giving music lessons. When Hemingway was an infant, Grace would sometimes dress him in a pink gingham dress and flowered hat to make him and his older sister, Marcelline, appear to be twins.

The Hemingways had summered on Walloon Lake in Petoskey, Michigan, the year before Ernest's birth. By the time he was born, they had purchased an acre of land and built a cabin on the lake. Grace christened the property "Windemere" in honor of her English heritage. The cabin served as the family's summer home, where Ernest first learned to hunt and fish and developed an appreciation for wild animals, and where he spent his first eighteen summers.

Ernest uttered his first sentence on St. Patrick's Day in 1901, and had already demonstrated a propensity for language by inventing nicknames for relatives and toys. He had also begun to behave like a man. According to his mother, when he was still less than three years old, Ernest proclaimed that he was "fraid [*sic*] of nothing" and would march about the house with a broken musket on his shoulder spouting stanzas from Lord Alfred Tennyson's "Charge of the Light Brigade."

In 1905, Grace Hemingway, against Ed's wishes, purchased a forty-acre farm across the lake from their summer cabin, arguing that the cabin had become too cramped for their growing family, which now included Ernest, Marcelline, and two younger sisters, Ursula and Madeline. (The family would eventually grow to six children with the birth of another sister, Carol, in 1911, and a brother, Leicester, in 1915.) Grace named the place Longfield Farm.

Grace also arranged for the sale of her father's house, the Hemingways' primary residence, and moved the family into a rented house while a new house was built at 600 North Kenilworth Avenue in Illinois. The Kenilworth house was larger and included a music room for Grace and a medical office for Ed. From his mother, who encouraged him to play the cello, Ernest gained a lifelong appreciation of classical music.

The day after his confirmation at the Third Congregational Church, Ernest wrote his first short story—a short piece entitled "My First Sea Vouge [*sic*]," which was based on a story his Uncle Tyley had told him. By 1912, Ernest had begun to experiment with poetry. He debuted on the stage in a school production of *Robin Hood*.

At Oak Park and River Forest High School, Ernest involved himself in a number of sports, including boxing, swimming, football, and track, but he was too small to excel in any activity except Rifle Club. However, he was a favorite among English teachers and his writing was regularly read in class. Much influenced by the satiric wit of Ring Lardner, who wrote for the *Chicago Tribune*, Ernest contributed regularly to the school literary magazine (*The Tabula*) and weekly newspaper (*The Trapeze*). His first published short stories appeared in *The Tabula* in 1916, when he

ERNEST HEMINGWAY'S PARENTS, ED AND GRACE, DOTED ON THEIR SON IN DIFFERENT WAYS. HIS FATHER INTRODUCED HIM TO THE JOYS OF THE OUTDOORS; HIS MOTHER, TO MUSIC AND THE ARTS.

was seventeen, the same year he witnessed his first prizefight and became an avid fan of boxing. He is listed in his senior high school yearbook as associate editor of *The Trapeze* and labeled "Class Prophet," along with the quote "None are to be found more clever than Ernie."

Hemingway's childhood is marked by two key elements: his talent for storytelling and his desire to cast himself as a masculine hero. At the age of five, he told his grandfather that he had single-handedly stopped a runaway horse. By the time he graduated from high school, he regularly embellished stories about himself, a tendency that would remain with him for the rest of his life.

Young Journalist

After graduating from high school and enjoying his last summer at Windemere, Hemingway moved to Kansas City where he earned fifteen dollars a week as a cub reporter for the *Kansas City Star*. The *Star* gave Hemingway his first lessons in professional writing. He received advice from seasoned journalists and benefited from the *Star*'s stylebook. Both provided him with the following guidelines for his writing:

> Limit your use of adjectives and
> avoid all hackneyed adjectives
> Avoid trite phrases
> Avoid superfluous words
> Tell an interesting narrative
> Use short sentences
> Start with short first paragraphs
> Use vigorous language
> Strive for smoothness
> Be positive, not negative

Hemingway claimed that it was while at the *Star* that he "learned to write a simple, declarative sentence." The lessons he learned there served him well throughout his writing career.

Hemingway's top interests while working for the *Star* in 1918 were his desire to learn to write and his interest in the Great War, later known as World War I. The Americans had recently entered the war, firing their first shots in France at the end of 1917. Hemingway was drawn to the action despite his father's prohibition against entering the war and his reported inability to enlist because of poor vision in his left eye. When he learned that other young men had enlisted in the American Field Service to drive ambulances for the Red Cross, he jumped at the chance to join the battle overseas. That service did not have the same restrictions as the U.S. military. On May 23, 1918, Hemingway shipped out, eventually arriving in Italy where he worked as an ambulance driver for the Red Cross.

War Wounds and First Love

Hemingway was full of boyish naiveté and enthusiasm when he arrived in Europe. He was anxious to see the war up close. The Red Cross assigned him to Section Four of the Ambulance Corps and housed him in Schio, Italy, seventy miles to the west of Venice, in a building that Hemingway and the other drivers jokingly referred to as the Schio Country Club. While there he met John Dos Passos, who, like Hemingway, would become a key literary figure of the postwar period in American literature.

Impatient for action, Hemingway was the first in line when Lieutenant Griffin asked for volunteers to man the canteens, which provided cigarettes, candy, and other personal items to soldiers closer to the battle lines. Hemingway was sent to the small village of Fossalta on the West Bank of the Piave River where Italian forces were entrenched. Austrian forces had dug in to the east. While bullets flew through the air and shells exploded, Hemingway rushed "cigarettes, chocolate, and postcards" to the soldiers fighting on the front.

Around midnight on July 8, 1918, Hemingway was delivering chocolate to the soldiers in the trenches when a "muzzle-loaded Austrian trench mortar" flew across the river and exploded a few feet from him. A soldier standing between Hemingway and the explosion was killed. Another standing close by lost both his legs. A third soldier was severely injured. Hemingway was knocked unconscious. When he came to, Hemingway, despite the hundreds of pieces of metal embedded in his legs, dragged the wounded soldier to the dugout where he could receive medical care. The man died.

As with nearly all of Hemingway's exploits, it is difficult to know with certainty everything that occurred because Hemingway frequently embellished and exaggerated many of the events of his life, particularly those involving bravery and masculinity. Nevertheless,

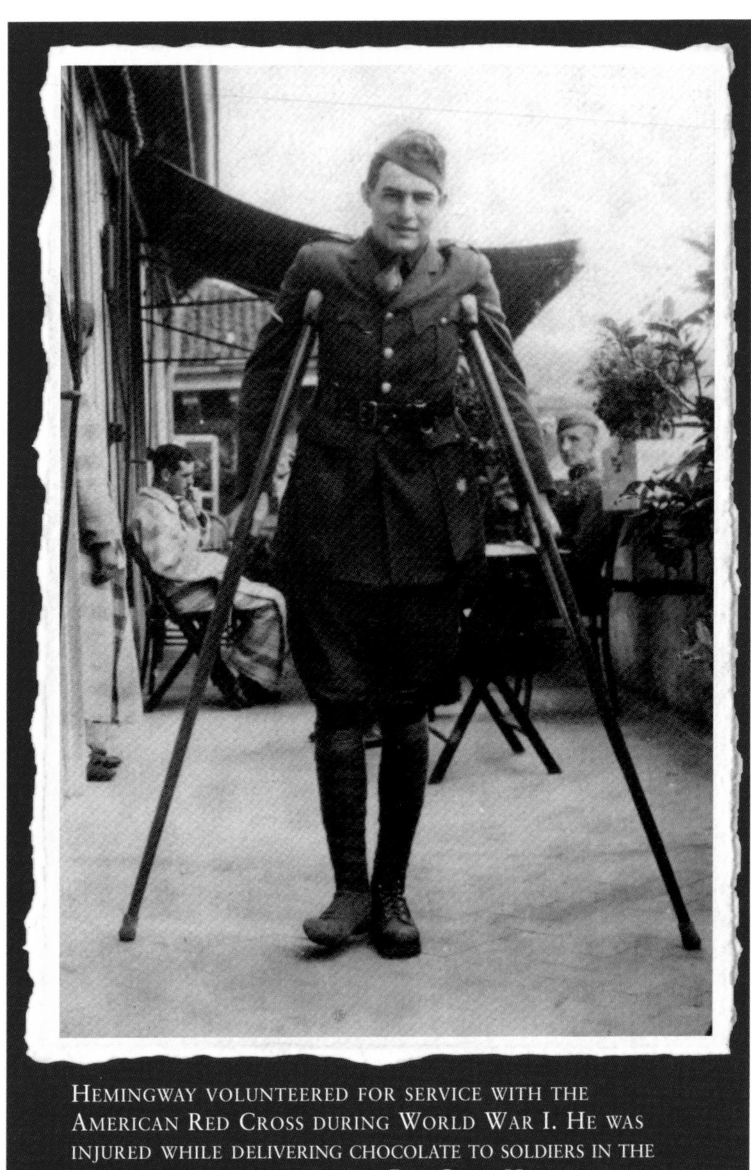

Hemingway volunteered for service with the American Red Cross during World War I. He was injured while delivering chocolate to soldiers in the trenches and ended up in the Red Cross Hospital in Milan in 1918.

Hemingway in this situation certainly acted bravely despite the risks to his own life. According to the American Red Cross's records, Hemingway had "received 237 separate wounds in his leg[s]. All but ten of these wounds . . . [were] superficial."

Hemingway's wounding in Fossalta represents the first major juncture in his life. He had proven his bravery in the trenches and had been honorably wounded without ending up with any permanent injury. The event fortified his confidence in his manhood and gave him a sense of personal strength, placing him above ordinary men. He was, after all, the first American to be wounded in Italy. As biographer Jeffrey Meyers phrased it: "Hemingway was able to transform what began as a commonplace distribution of chocolate and cigarettes into something glorious and noble."

Hemingway was first sent to a field hospital in Fornaci, where he claimed a priest formally baptized him in the Catholic faith (a tale that turned out to be false), and was then transported to a base hospital in Milan. In the Milan hospital, Hemingway was in good spirits, drinking brandy, wine, and cognac, and digging shrapnel out of his leg with a penknife. His only concern seemed to be that they might amputate his leg.

One of his nurses was an American woman named Agnes von Kurowsky. Hemingway fell in love with Agnes, who was seven years older. She would eventually become the model for Catherine Barkley in *A Farewell to Arms*. In October 1918, Agnes transferred to a hospital in Florence where there had been a breakout of influenza. Hemingway and Agnes exchanged loving letters, meeting on occasion, and there were hints that they might someday marry.

Hemingway arrived back in New York on January 21, 1919, pleased to discover that he had achieved a modicum of fame because he had been wounded on the front lines in Italy. Agnes's letters became less frequent, until in March

While in the hospital during World War I, Hemingway met and fell in love with his nurse, Agnes von Kurowsky. She jilted him in favor of another man.

she confessed that she had fallen in love with another man, and broke off her relationship with Hemingway. Hemingway's wounding in Italy is significant for at least two reasons. First, as Arthur Waldhorn notes, "the explosion that shattered Hemingway's body metaphorically penetrated his mind too." Hemingway was changed as a result of the incident and those changes shaped his writing. After he was wounded, for example, Hemingway struggled with insomnia and "a total inability to sleep in the dark," a condition that is echoed in many of his heroes. Jake Barnes in *The Sun Also Rises*, Frederic Henry in *A Farewell to Arms,* and Nick Adams in his stories, all suffer from insomnia. Scholar Philip Young argues that much of Hemingway's later life and writing were attempts to deal with the trauma he suffered in the war. Second, the wounding led to his hospitalization and subsequent love affair with Agnes. Hemingway was devastated by the breakup with Agnes and many scholars argue that this emotional blow left Hemingway with ambivalent feelings toward women and contributed to his mixed presentation of female characters in his fiction.

After his break with Agnes, Hemingway spent a brief time lounging about his parents' house in Oak Park, until his mother insisted he stop goofing off and put him out of the house. He moved to Chicago, where he wrote articles for the *Toronto Star*. In 1920, he met Elizabeth Hadley Richardson. Like his mother, Hadley was a musician. Like Agnes, Hadley was older than Hemingway—eight years older. Hadley and Hemingway married on September 3, 1921.

Unable to find a market for his short stories, Hemingway had very little money, but Hadley had a trust fund that provided them with $3,000 (equivalent to about $27,000 today). They originally planned to move to Italy where Hemingway could write, but changed their minds when author Sherwood Anderson advised them to head for Paris, which he claimed was the only place for a writer.

Paris and Beyond

Sherwood Anderson wrote letters of introduction to a number of American expatriates living in Paris. These included Gertrude Stein, who lived with her lifelong companion, Alice B. Toklas; Sylvia Beach, who ran Shakespeare and Company, a bookshop frequented by important literary figures such as James Joyce; and Ezra Pound, a powerful poet and key figure in the literary movements of their time.

On January 9, 1922, the Hemingways moved into a small apartment at 74, rue du Cardinal Lemoine. While Hadley kept house, Hemingway reveled in his literary and personal freedom. He set out to establish new criteria for his writing, claiming that "all you have to do is write one true sentence . . . the truest sentence you know . . . [a] true simple declarative sentence."

Hemingway's literary goal was to clear away from his writing all remnants of superfluous ornamentation and to directly record the world as it actually was. Hemingway was one of many young, modern writers who wanted to discover new methods for producing stories and poetry. They found many traditional views of art pretentious, outside the realm of lived experience, and unsuited to explain the world that had given rise to World War I—the war to end all wars.

Many important people saw promise in Hemingway. Pound praised his poetry and helped Hemingway publish his poetry and stories. (In exchange, Hemingway gave Pound boxing lessons.) Stein, whom Hemingway and Hadley met in March, was very impressed by the young writer and advised him about his writing.

Hemingway still wrote for the *Toronto Star*, sending articles on a broad range of subjects back to North America. He covered the Genoa Conference of 1922, a gathering in Italy of thirty-four nations to address damages to the European financial and commerce system caused by World War I. He interviewed Benito Mussolini, who had just begun to acquire the power and influence that would enable him to become dictator of Italy in 1922. He also covered less formidable topics, such as tuna fishing and tourism.

Hemingway regularly visited Shakespeare and Company, a bookstore popular among other American expatriates, and literary and artistic figures. The surrealist artist Man Ray, himself a regular visitor, took photographs of many of the other writers and artists for the store. Sylvia Beach published the first edition of *Ulysses* by James Joyce, the Irish novelist who frequented the store. Pound staked out a favorite chair near the stove that heated the ground floor. It was through Beach that Hemingway met Robert McAlmon, who would become the publisher of Hemingway's first book. After he died, a book of his essays about his expatriate days and the people he met in Paris was published in *A Moveable Feast.*

Through his many developing connections, Hemingway began to publish the occasional short story and poem. He considered the writing of prose and poetry "real" writing and relished every opportunity to work on nonjournalistic pieces. In 1922, Hadley took a train to Lausanne, Switzerland, to meet Hemingway. She carried with her a valise containing all the writing Hemingway had done since arriving in Paris, which she was bringing to him so he could work. On the way, the valise was stolen. Hemingway was shattered by the loss.

In 1923, Hadley became pregnant with their first child. During the pregnancy, they visited Spain for the first time. In Pamplona, Hemingway was introduced to bullfighting, which would become a lifelong avocation for him and would inspire the writing of numerous stories and one book. Hemingway was impressed with the manliness of the bullring and the bravery of the matadors. After returning to Paris, the Hemingways decided they would leave Paris so that Hadley could give birth on North American soil. On October 10, Hadley gave birth to their

After first wife Hadley gave birth to their son in 1923, John Hadley Nicanor, they moved back to Europe. In 1926, they visited Austria.

son—John Hadley Nicanor (Bumby) Hemingway. That same year, Hemingway's first book, *Three Stories and Ten Poems*, was published.

In January 1924, tired of journalism and missing Paris, Hemingway and his family headed back to Europe. Gertrude Stein and Alice B. Toklas became Bumby's godmothers when he was christened at St. Luke's Episcopal Church, and Hemingway began to focus on serious writing. He completed many short stories in 1924, including a long one called "Big Two-Hearted River", whose protagonist was Nick Adams, a fictional counterpart to Hemingway as a youth and a recurring character in his stories. When he had written enough stories to make up a book-length collection (which he titled *In Our Time*), he managed, with the help of writer Don Ogden Stewart, to acquire a publication deal with Boni and Liveright, a New York publishing house. He received an advance of two hundred dollars. The story "Up in Michigan" was deleted from the collection because its sexual subject matter was judged too racy.

Shortly after signing the deal on *In Our Time*, Hemingway was contacted by Maxwell Perkins, an important editor at Charles Scribners Sons. Perkins worked with a number of important writers, including F. Scott Fitzgerald, bestselling author of *The Great Gatsby* and popular short stories, and Thomas Wolfe, author of *Look Homeward Angel.* Although Hemingway had already granted Boni and Liveright options on his next two books, he was encouraged by the developing relationship with Perkins and felt that he was finally establishing himself as a writer.

Hemingway met F. Scott Fitzgerald in May 1925, when Fitzgerald (already a famous writer) introduced himself at The Dingo, a bar on rue Delambre where Hemingway was drinking. It was Fitzgerald who had interested Perkins in Hemingway's work.

After one false start, Hemingway began a novel inspired by his third trip to the bullfights of Spain. He completed the book on September 21, 1925. Its working title had

BULLFIGHTS WOULD BECOME KEY TO BOTH HEMINGWAY'S LIFE AND WRITING. THE SPANISH BULLFIGHTS HE WATCHED IN THE 1920S INSPIRED *THE SUN ALSO RISES.*

been *Fiesta*. Now he considered other possibilities, including *River to the Sea*, *Two Lie Together*, and even *The Lost Generation*, based on the phrase coined by Stein referring to the young, disillusioned men and women left over after the war. He settled on *The Sun Also Rises*, which he borrowed from a passage in Ecclesiastes, a book in the Old Testament of the Bible.

Fame

In Our Time came out in October. The reviews were good. The *New York Times* review said of Hemingway that "He looks out upon the world without prejudice or preconception and records with precision and economy, and an almost terrifying immediacy, exactly what he sees.

His short stories, sketches, anecdotes and epigrams are triumphs of sheer objectivity."

Emboldened by the good reception *In Our Time* received, Hemingway wrote a novel that parodied Sherwood Anderson's recent work. Anderson had provided invaluable help to Hemingway when he was starting out. Hemingway's writing had often been compared to Anderson's, but Hemingway had tired of the comparison and did not hold back from ridiculing the author in the new novel, *The Torrents of Spring*. Striking back at people who had befriended and aided him along the way would become a frequent occurrence with Hemingway, and he would, during his life, criticize even his closest early allies, such as Stein and Fitzgerald.

Hemingway sent *The Torrents of Spring* to Boni and Liveright, to whom Hemingway was contractually obligated and who published Sherwood Anderson's work. Horace Liveright was also Anderson's friend. The publishing house passed on Hemingway's novel, effectively releasing him from his contract and freeing him to publish the book with Perkins at Scribners. Some speculate that Hemingway may have planned the novel as a way to get out of his contract with Boni and Liveright after the success of *In Our Time*.

The book came out in April 1926, but Scribners preferred to promote the soon-to-be-published *The Sun Also Rises* as Hemingway's "first novel." The publisher simply referred to *The Torrents of Spring* as a "burlesque" and a "satire" of Sherwood Anderson's *Dark Laughter*. The review in the *New York Times* praised *Torrents*, calling it a "full-blooded comedy" that "contributes to that thoughtful gayety which true wit should inspire."

When *The Sun Also Rises* was published later in 1926, Hemingway's reputation as a writer continued to grow. Meanwhile, he met and began an affair with Pauline Pfeiffer, a well-heeled socialite, a fashion editor for *Vogue* magazine, and a close personal friend of Hadley. At the time, Pauline was thirty and Hemingway was twenty-six. Although Hadley suspected that Hemingway and Pauline were romantically involved, Pauline and her sister Jinny joined the Hemingways, Scott and Zelda Fitzgerald, and Gerald and Sara Murphy (wealthy friends of the Fitzgeralds) on a trip to Pamplona. After the trip, Hadley confronted Hemingway and he confessed to his relationship with Pauline. Hadley agreed to grant him a divorce, but only if he and Pauline would separate for one hundred days. If they still wanted to pursue their relationship after the separation, Hadley would not stand in their way.

Gerald Murphy loaned Hemingway his flat in Paris and gave him four hundred dollars to help ease the transition back to single life. Hemingway, who would often regret leaving Hadley, would eventually blame Murphy (and by extension, all wealthy people) for his divorce, saying, "I . . . hated these rich because they had backed me and encouraged me when I was doing wrong." Hemingway typically deflected blame whenever he was at fault or had not performed to his own expectations. Years later he would even blame Pauline for intentionally seducing him away from Hadley. However, he did say to Bill Bird, when Bird asked why they were divorcing, "Because I'm a son of a ——," and he felt guilty enough at the time to assign all royalties from *The Sun Also Rises* to Hadley and his son, Bumby.

After the hundred-day separation, Hemingway and Pauline were married in a Catholic ceremony on May 10, 1927. They honeymooned in Grau-du-Roi at the mouth of the Rhône River. In 1927, a second collection of short stories was published under the title *Men Without Women* and sold nearly 20,000 copies by April.

Key West

In 1928, Hemingway and his new wife moved back to the United States and settled in Key West, Florida, a harbor town well-suited to Hemingway's preference for casual living. He spent many hours in Key West fishing and drinking at Sloppy Joe's Bar. In the summer, Hemingway and Pauline, who was pregnant, traveled to Kansas City where the hospitals were better. She gave birth to Patrick Hemingway on June 28. After Pauline had recovered, the Hemingways returned to Key West.

Soon after, Hemingway traveled to New York to see his first son, Bumby. At the train station in New Jersey, Hemingway received a telegram informing him that his father had died. Ed Hemingway had become increasingly despondent over physical ailments and financial difficulties and had shot himself. Ed's suicide was one of many that would haunt Hemingway. Hadley's father had also committed suicide and there would be more suicides in Hemingway's future, including his own.

The Hemingways returned to Paris in 1929 where Hemingway worked on magazine proofs of his next novel, *A Farewell to Arms*, which was being serialized in *Scribners Magazine*. But Paris had lost some of its earlier charm for Hemingway. By 1930 he and Pauline were living in Key West again, driven back partly by the stock market crash in 1929 and the subsequent devaluation of the U.S. dollar against the franc. In 1930, they took a trip to the L-T Ranch in Wyoming, where Hemingway was thrilled to hunt bull elk and bear, and to fish.

In November, after camping out in Yellowstone National Park, Hemingway was in an automobile accident outside Billings, Montana. He shattered his right arm. Because Hemingway wrote his first drafts with a pen (and he was right-handed), he was unable to work. The break was painful and took months to heal.

Back in Key West, Hemingway recovered. He continued to host fishing expeditions for friends, which he had done since discovering Key West. By April 1931, Pauline was expecting another child. The Hemingways bought a house at 907 Whitehead Street with funds provided by Pauline's Uncle Gus as a gift for his niece.

In the summer, Hemingway, who was now working on a book about bullfighting (*Death in the Afternoon*), headed back to Spain. Pauline, Patrick, and their nanny followed. Hemingway found Spain in the throes of political unrest. The Spanish king, Alfonso XIII, was forced into exile by Republican forces and the country was moving toward civil war, one that Hemingway predicted in a letter to author John Dos Passos.

Toward the end of 1931, the Hemingways were back in Kansas City where Pauline gave birth to Gregory Hancock Hemingway, Hemingway's third son, on the morning of November 12. In January, Hemingway delivered *Death in the Afternoon* to Perkins at Scribners.

In 1932, Hemingway put off for a second time a much-desired hunting trip to Africa and the Hemingways once again visited the L-T Ranch in Wyoming. In September, *Death in the Afternoon* was published. It received mixed reviews. By now, the reputation of Hemingway the man was keeping pace with the reputation of Hemingway the writer, and stories abounded about his exploits. Though some were accurate, many were exaggerated, partly by Hollywood studios promoting films based on his works and partly by Hemingway himself, who seemed to be crafting his image as a heroic, manly figure as carefully as he crafted his writing.

In 1933, Hemingway's third collection of short stories, *Winner Take Nothing*, was published. As the year ended, Hemingway began his long-planned safari to Africa. He was impressed with the continent, which he found beautiful and full of game. Hemingway hunted a wide variety of animals, such as gazelle, impala, kongoni, lion, rhinoceros, guinea fowl, kudu, leopard, and sandgrouse. Suffering from dysentery and "a prolapse of the lower intestine," he was flown to Nairobi for two weeks of treatment, after which he rejoined the safari.

Ernest Hemingway left his first wife, Hadley, for Pauline Pfeiffer (R), with whom Hadley had been friends.

The trip thrilled Hemingway, who was charmed by the focus on courage, dignity, and masculine pride that hunting big game in Africa enabled. Facing the savage wonders of nature placed Hemingway in his element.

While returning from the safari, Hemingway heard that the island of Bimini, forty-five miles from Miami, offered lush fishing. Back in Key West, Hemingway bought a 38-foot boat to travel to the island. He christened it the *Pilar*. Between fishing trips, he worked on a book about Africa.

He felt that his own writing was going very well. He believed that in the past year he had gained greater control over his narrative technique and that he had written "absolutely truly—absolutely with no faking or cheating of any kind." Despite an ego that many considered enlarged, Hemingway was indeed writing well.

Hemingway spent much of 1935 fishing for tuna and marlin off the waters of Bimini. His behavior could often get out of hand and he was known to occasionally bully people. He always seemed interested in proving his manhood. At one point in Bimini, when the fishing was poor, he offered two hundred fifty dollars to any "Negro who could stay in the ring with him for three three-minute rounds."

That year Scribners published his novel *Green Hills of Africa*. C. G. Poore, who reviewed the book for the *New York Times*, praised Hemingway's writing, saying it is "better than ever, richer, deeper." Although he claimed the book was the "best-written story of big game hunting anywhere," he called for Hemingway to write about "a novel of vast and striking scope instead of wasting time calling shots on the kudu."

Hemingway, at thirty-four, was famous for his writing and his personal exploits, but some felt that fame did not suit the writer. The poet Archibald MacLeish, a fellow expatriate and longtime friend of Hemingway's, felt that Hemingway's ego had grown out of proportion.

Hemingway was also critical of other writers and friends, including MacLeish, whom he claimed was too involved in politics. Hemingway criticized Fitzgerald's *Tender Is the Night*, claiming that he had "cheated too damn much" in writing the book. His criticism wounded Fitzgerald, who idolized Hemingway and was struggling with his talent and alcoholism.

Though Hemingway continued to receive praise for his work, he was also critiqued. Ivan Kashkeen's (sometimes spelled Kashkin) essay, "Ernest Hemingway: The Tragedy of Craftsmanship," characterized Hemingway's work as a mask that concealed "tragic disharmony inside Hemingway, a psychic discord that had brought him to the edge of disintegration." Kashkeen made the important observation that "again and again he [Hemingway] was writing of the end—the end of love, the end of life, the end of hope, the end of all." Hemingway thought Kashkeen's comments were perceptive.

In 1936, Hemingway worked on his next collection of short stories and on what would become his next novel. In December, while hanging out at Sloppy Joe's Bar in Key West, he met Martha Gellhorn, who was there on vacation with her mother and brother. Gellhorn, like Hemingway, was a published author and ambitious journalist. She was friends with Eleanor Roosevelt and the president. Hemingway, who could be charming when the mood struck him, became cozy with the family. When the mother and the brother left, the daughter stayed on in Key West. When she left in January of 1937, Hemingway and she arranged a meeting in Miami.

Spain, China, and Cuba

Later that year, Hemingway and Gellhorn met in Spain where they were both covering the Spanish Civil War (1936–1939). Gellhorn was a war correspondent for *Collier's Weekly* and Hemingway reported for the North

American News Alliance (NANA). They both operated out of the same hotel in Madrid, where many of Hemingway's friends and acquaintances also stayed.

While in Madrid, Hemingway got involved with director Joris Ivens's documentary film project about the war: *The Spanish Earth*. Hemingway eventually provided the voice for the documentary, which was to have been narrated by Orson Welles, and also promoted the film, whose profits would be used to fund ambulances in the war effort. He visited the front lines in Spain a second time toward the end of 1937. While there, his next novel, *To Have and Have Not*, was published. It sold well, but received mixed reviews. The bad reviews enraged him, as did all criticism of his work.

Hemingway used his experiences in Spain as material for his first play, *The Fifth Column*, a highly autobiographical piece about a war correspondent named Philip Rawlings who, as Carlos Baker notes, engaged in behavior that "included much drinking and fighting, many irrational quarrels, frequent assertion of his manhood, and a determination not to surrender to the domination of women."

Despite Pauline's attempts to salvage their marriage, by 1938 it was essentially over, though they would not officially divorce until 1940. In 1939, Hemingway's play, *The Fifth Column*, was published along with a collection of his short stories in a book titled *The Fifth Column and the First Forty-nine Stories*.

In 1939, Hemingway took the *Pilar* down to Cuba. Gellhorn soon followed. She set up housekeeping near Havana in an estate called La Finca Vigía. While she wrote about her time in Prague before the Nazi invasion, Hemingway worked on his next novel, *For Whom the Bell Tolls*, which was inspired by his experiences during the Spanish Civil War. On Christmas Eve, Hemingway removed personal items from the house in Key West, including books and "several paintings by Miro, Léger, and Juan Gris," and made permanent his residence in Cuba.

In the summer of 1940, Hemingway completed *For Whom the Bell Tolls*. His divorce from Pauline became final on November 4 and Martha Gellhorn became his third wife on November 21. The marriage was perhaps doomed from the start, as Martha's mother suspected when she tried to convince her daughter not to marry Hemingway. Gellhorn had no intention of abandoning her career to spend her life as a handmaiden to the famous Ernest Hemingway. She was a dynamic woman, a skilled journalist, a powerful writer, and no less afraid of the front lines than Hemingway. David Sandison summed up the differences between them:

> The two were, in fact, very different writers. Martha was, and would remain, a sharp-eyed observer and a gifted journalist capable of stripping away pretence and propaganda to inform her readers what the scores really were. Hemingway was a world-famous celebrity who, more often than not, used his fame to pronounce with assumed authority, generalizing with impunity and often settling for the well-rounded good-sounding phrase when a less adorned line would have served better.

These differences were apparent in the dispatches they sent back from China where they went to cover the Sino-Japanese War. Gellhorn wrote of the "squalor and disease . . . the ubiquity of opium dens and the abuse of young girls sold into prostitution," while Hemingway wrote about subjects such as "the sensations of drinking bird wine and snake wine."

In 1942, Hemingway engaged in two endeavors in Cuba that many would deem bizarre. First, he organized a group of men in Cuba to become spies, enlisting some fishermen, noblemen, waiters, and others to act as informants in the war effort. Hemingway called the group the "Crook Factory." Once a week, he delivered a report to Bob Joyce at the embassy office in Havana. These reports were of questionable use to the U.S. military efforts. When Hemingway grew dissatisfied with his spy network, he arranged to have the *Pilar* armed with machine guns, grenades, and bombs, and received permission to travel the areas around Cuba. These areas were frequented by German submarines. Hemingway planned to lure the submarines to approach the *Pilar* where Hemingway and a band of his local fans were prepared to use the weapons to destroy them. Most of the *Pilar's* sub-hunting was followed by "noisy drinking parties at all hours," which disturbed Gellhorn. She considered the whole business a ridiculous excuse to drink, circumvent fuel rationing, and get to go fishing while playing at war.

Toward the end of 1943, Gellhorn, who had finished work on her novel, set off for England to cover World War II for *Collier's*, leaving Hemingway alone in Cuba. Hemingway was writing very little. In 1944, Gellhorn arranged for Hemingway to get passage to Europe.

Another War, Another Wife

Hemingway met Mary Welsh shortly after arriving in London in 1944. Mary was a feature writer for the *Daily Express* and the wife of an Australian reporter writing for the *Daily Mail*. Mary was an established professional woman, a woman of accomplishment who had worked for the London bureaus of *Time*, *Life*, and *Fortune*. When Hemingway was hospitalized after an automobile accident, Martha visited him, but found his exploits childish. The poet John Pudney's impressions of Hemingway were that "he was a fellow obsessed with playing the part of Ernest Hemingway . . . a cardboard figure."

Hemingway was present for the D-Day invasion on June 6, 1944, when 160,000 troops landed on the beaches of Normandy. He watched from an observation ship. Martha, who had gotten aboard a hospital ship, managed to come ashore with the soldiers, a sore point with Hemingway, who didn't like to be upstaged by anyone, much less a woman.

Hemingway was uncomfortable with mere journalistic observation and was anxious to involve himself more in the conflict. He often overstepped the acceptable boundaries set up for war correspondents. At one point, he took charge of a band of partisans and set them up as guardians of the town of Rambouillet. He interrogated people and often went about without his correspondent's insignia, a violation of the Geneva agreement, which required journalists to wear their insignia at all times. Hemingway entered Paris in August during its liberation and set himself up at the Ritz, where he drank champagne and waited for the Allies to enter the city. Mary Welsh arrived later, and they continued their courtship.

In October, the military held a hearing to determine if Hemingway had engaged in illegal activities by commanding troops, removing his insignia, and engaging in military activities rather than writing dispatches. Hemingway was forced to lie about his activities or face losing his war correspondent credentials and being shipped back to the United States. He was exonerated. That same month Martha decided she'd had enough and asked for a divorce.

In March 1945, when Hemingway left Europe, he was suffering from severe headaches, presumably the result of several head injuries he had received in two years. He was impatient to start writing again. He returned to La Finca Vigía in Cuba where he was shortly joined by Mary, but he had trouble getting back to writing. On December 21, he was officially divorced from

Martha Gellhorn, Hemingway's third wife, was an influential journalist whose reputation still shines long after her death. Hemingway did not enjoy the competition.

Martha. He married Mary (who, unlike Martha, was willing to abandon her career to be his wife) on March 14, 1946, in Havana. He also began working on *The Garden of Eden*.

Hemingway's health was in decline. In August 1947, he began to be plagued by a buzzing inside his head. He was overweight and had abnormally high blood pressure. Amid struggles with his health, his relationships, his reputation, and his writing, he finally managed to complete his next novel, *Across the River and Into the Trees*, which was published in 1950. The book did not receive many favorable reviews. Tellingly, John O'Hara's review in the *New York Times* allots more space to discussing Hemingway the man and the importance of his literary career than it spends examining his latest novel.

At the end of 1950, Hemingway's ability to write returned. He worked on his "sea novel," part of which would become *The Old Man and the Sea*, based on a story he had been told in 1935. Another section would become the posthumously published *Islands in the Stream*.

Scribners published part of the larger manuscript as a short novel, titled *The Old Man and the Sea*, in 1952. Nearly everyone who read the work realized that Hemingway had produced something marvelous. Author William Faulkner said in a review, "Time may show it to be the best single piece by any of us." Hemingway also realized that there was something special about *The Old Man and the Sea*. In a *Time* magazine review, Hemingway is quoted as saying, "I have had to read it now over 200 times and every time it does something to me. It's as though I had gotten finally what I had been working for all my life." The book was awarded the Pulitzer Prize for fiction in 1953.

That same year, Hemingway returned to Africa for another safari, this time with Mary. In 1954, he hired a plane to fly Mary and him over the scenic landscape. Near Murchinson Falls, the pilot maneuvered to avoid a bird and a telegraph wire hit the propeller. The plane went down on Ugandan soil. Mary was in shock and Hemingway's shoulder was sprained, but no one was seriously injured. However, they were in danger. The following day, Hemingway signaled a boat on the river. They were rescued and taken to Butiaba where they learned that the plane wreckage had been spotted and reports had circulated claiming that the Hemingways had died in the crash. But their troubles weren't over yet. When taking off from the Butiaba airport, the plane that was to take them to Entebbe burst into flames on takeoff. The pilot kicked out a window and he and Mary climbed to safety.

FOURTH AND FINAL WIFE MARY WELSH WAS ALSO A JOURNALIST WHEN SHE MET HEMINGWAY, BUT SHE (*SECOND FROM LEFT*) ABANDONED HER CAREER TO TAKE CARE OF HIM.

Hemingway's door was jammed and he had to smash it open, badly injuring his head. They were driven fifty miles to Masindi, and then to Entebbe. By then, news services worldwide were reporting their miraculous survival.

The two consecutive plane crashes added to the long list of injuries Hemingway had endured in his life. He suffered a "severe concussion, ruptured liver, spleen, and kidney, temporary loss of vision in the left eye, loss of hearing in the left ear, a crushed vertebra, a sprained right arm and shoulder, a sprained left leg, paralysis of the sphincter, and first degree burns on his face, arms, and head."

Later in 1954, Hemingway won the Nobel Prize in Literature, which had previously eluded him. His ailing health prevented him from receiving the award in person. He sent along a written statement to be read at the awards ceremony. In it, Hemingway said that "Writing, at its best, is a lonely life."

In 1955, Hemingway wrote a new will leaving everything to Mary, whom he trusted to take care of his children. Over the next few years, he continued to write, though the quality of his work had diminished somewhat since *The Old Man and the Sea*. He still struggled with his health. In 1958, he left Cuba and moved to a rented house in Ketchum, Idaho, in Sun Valley. In 1959, just before a trip to Spain, he purchased the Topping House in Ketchum.

According to Carlos Baker, Hemingway's biographer, the first hint that Hemingway's mind might be slipping came on June 1, 1960. Hemingway had returned to his home in Ketchum and had been working on a long manuscript about bullfighting for *Life* magazine. He wrote in a letter to his longtime friend Juanito Quintana that the work he had been doing had "confused his brain." He returned to Spain for one more visit, but it was clear to everyone that Hemingway's ability to reason was suffering. Mary coaxed him back to Ketchum with difficulty.

Toward the end of the year, he was hospitalized, first at the Mayo Clinic and then at St. Mary's Hospital in Rochester, Minnesota. His many years of heavy drinking had taken their toll on his liver and he was suffering from high blood pressure, hypertension, and severe depression. He received shock treatments at St. Mary's. In January 1961, he was released from St. Mary's and returned to Ketchum, where he struggled to control his drinking and diet and return to work. However, by February he had stopped writing and fallen back into despair.

One morning in April, Mary found Hemingway with a shotgun. With the help of his doctor, she got the shotgun away from him and placed him in Sun Valley Hospital.

They decided to take him back to the Mayo Clinic, but while at home to pick up some clothes, Hemingway grabbed a shotgun and pointed it at his throat. Don Anderson, a local friend of the Hemingways, and the nurse who was with him, managed to get the gun away from him.

Hemingway was readmitted to the hospital for treatment. In June, he convinced his doctors that he was well enough to be released. He was released on June 26, and back in Ketchum by June 30. On the morning of Sunday, July 2, 1961, Hemingway went downstairs, retrieved a shotgun that Mary had locked away, loaded two shells, walked to the foyer, put the gun to his forehead, and pulled the trigger.

Chapter 2

Historical Events and Movements

Expatriates and The Lost Generation

Anyone taking on the serious study of Ernest Hemingway and his works will inevitably run across the terms "expatriate" and "the lost generation." The term "expatriate" refers to Americans living in foreign lands, and does not always imply dissatisfaction with America, although some expatriates, such as Ezra Pound, were greatly dissatisfied with American politics.

Many of Hemingway's American literary contemporaries were expatriates. Among them were Pound, Gertrude Stein, John Dos Passos, Henry Miller, F. Scott Fitzgerald, Malcolm Cowley, and T. S. Eliot. Eliot eventually gave up his U.S. citizenship altogether and became a British subject.

Hemingway spent much of his life living outside the United States. He spent a great deal of his time in France, Switzerland, Spain, and Italy, but he spent more time living in Cuba than any other foreign country.

American expatriates were particularly drawn to Paris in the 1920s for two reasons: first, a large community of young writers and artists could be found there, and second, the exchange rates were extremely favorable. Americans living in Paris got more buying power for their dollars than they would have received in the United States.

"The Lost Generation" is a term coined by Gertrude Stein and used in direct reference to Hemingway. It refers to the young men and women who were "blasted by the World War" (World War I). These young men and women were disillusioned with the inability of political bodies to insulate the world against war and rejected the rigid expectations of American business. The artists rejected traditional forms and sought to alter both the form and content of art and literature. Hemingway was at the heart of this movement.

Modern Period in American Literature

Opinions vary greatly on just about every aspect of the modern period in American literature, from when it began and ended to which characteristics it possessed. Nevertheless, a general understanding of the period can be gleaned from the large amount of attention the period and its terminology have received.

The modern period in American literature falls loosely between the beginning of World War I in 1914 and the end of World War II in 1945 (some estimates run as late as 1960). The writing of the period was marked by the following characteristics, though no single work or author employed them all:

1. An intentional turn away from traditional literary techniques, such as rhyme and set meter, and an increased experimentation with form and subject matter.
2. A unique type of imagination that was more self-oriented, operating under the principle that "we create the world in the act of perceiving it."
3. "A sense of alienation, loss, and despair."
4. "A rejection of history and the society of whose fabrication history is a record."
5. A rejection of "traditional values and assumptions" and the language used to "sanction and communicate" them.
6. A preference for the unconscious and the internal life of the mind.
7. A privileging of the "dense and often unordered reality" over the "practical and systematic."
8. Experimentation with "language, form, symbol, and myth."

Works generally associated with the modern period in American literature reflect dissatisfaction with the ideas and methods of previous generations and the attempt to refashion literature into something more vibrant and more relevant to the age following World War I. Hemingway is a central figure in this movement.

Hemingway's Wars

World War I

World War I, also called The Great War, the First World War, and The War to End All Wars, marked a significant change in the way societies waged war. The conflict was triggered in 1914 (Hemingway was fifteen) when the heir to the Austro-Hungarian throne, Archduke Ferdinand, was assassinated. Although many other factors helped fuel the war, Austria-Hungary, Germany, and Turkey used the event to launch a push into France. Their initial plan was to encircle Paris. They failed. France, Russia, and Great Britain fiercely fought against their intrusion.

The war was fought primarily on the Western Front, a moving line that stretched across Western Europe from the English Channel to Switzerland. The battles were fought in trenches, with each side struggling to gain ground on the other. Hemingway was wounded at the age of nineteen on the front lines where trench warfare was raging in the town of Fossalta, Italy.

World War I was unique in a number of important ways. It was particularly brutal. The industrial age had provided the world with war machinery capable of inflicting tremendous damage—bombs, tanks, machine guns, and chemical weapons. The cost of life was high. Thirty-two million soldiers were killed or injured during the four years of the war. However, because the war involved most countries in the region and entire populations, civilians also died in large numbers. Around sixty-two million people died during the conflict, of whom about half were civilians.

Ernest Hemingway covered the Spanish Civil War as a journalist. In 1937, he was photographed with Loyalist soldiers on the front lines.

By the end of the war in 1918, most major countries in the world were involved, including Greece, Belgium, Japan, Italy, Portugal, and the United States, which had joined the conflict in 1917, the last year of the war.

Spanish Civil War

The Spanish Civil War began on July 17, 1936, when supporters of the Nationalist Front, who had lost the last election, plotted to overthrow the elected Popular Front government led by President Manuel Azaña. European communists and socialists formed brigades and met in Spain to help defend the Popular Front ("Loyalists"). Men from a variety of left-wing organizations joined them, as did some members of the Spanish Army's Peninsular Army. On the other side ("Nationalists"), General Francisco Franco, a fascist (one who believes in authoritarian rule), flew the Army of Africa back to Spain to overthrow the government (the Army of Africa was composed of soldiers of the Spanish Army and Spanish Foreign Legion). The working class revolted against

Franco's attempted coup and the country became divided between the Loyalist working class and the Nationalists.

Hemingway, who covered the war as a correspondent, sided with the Loyalists and opposed fascism. This motivated him to work on two documentaries, *Spain in Flames* and *The Spanish Earth*, and to help raise funds in America for the Loyalist efforts in Spain.

Franco received weapons and support from both Hitler's Germany and Mussolini's Italy during the war. In 1939, after the fall of Madrid, where Hemingway had spent most of his time, the war ended and Franco's brutal dictatorship began.

Sino-Japanese War

The Sino-Japanese War that Hemingway covered as a correspondent (which was actually the second Sino-Japanese War, the first having occurred from 1894–1895) began in 1937 with the Marco Polo Bridge Incident. The Japanese had been systematically working their way into China for a number of years. In July, a battle ensued between Japanese and Chinese at the Lugou Bridge, also called Marco Polo Bridge, near Beijing, which started the war.

Hemingway and Martha Gellhorn were in China from January to May of 1941, but never saw action. The war ended along with World War II in 1945 after the bombing of Hiroshima and Nagasaki.

World War II

World War II began in 1939. That year, Germany invaded Czechoslovakia and then Poland. On September 3, Great Britain and France, who were allies of Poland, declared war on Germany. Although the Soviet Union had pledged its support to France and Britain in April, it signed a non-aggression act with Germany in August and it too entered Poland in September.

In 1940, Hitler launched offensives into France and Belgium. The fascist Italian dictator, Benito Mussolini,

THE SPANISH CIVIL WAR WAS A CAUSE CÉLÈBRE FOR MANY AMERICANS WHO BELIEVED IN THE RIGHTS OF THE OPPRESSED. THIS POSTER SHOWS BOTH COMMUNIST AND ANARCHIST COLORS AND EMBLEMS.

declared war against the Allies in June, the same month that Germany marched into Paris. In July, the Luftwaffe began its assault on Britain, and in September, Japan signed a pact with Germany and Italy. In 1941, Bulgaria joined forces with Germany, Italy, and Japan, and invaded Yugoslavia along with German and Italian forces. In June, Finland and Hungary declared war on the Soviet Union, and the Soviet Union signed an agreement of mutual aid with Great Britain. German forces moved into the Soviet Union while Japanese troops invaded Thailand, Malaya, and the Philippines. When Japanese forces attacked Pearl Harbor on December 7, America entered into the war, joining forces with Britain, France, and the Soviet Union.

In 1943, Mussolini was taken out of office and placed in prison by the Italian king, Vittorio Emanuele III, who had taken charge of the army. In October, Italy declared war on Germany. On June 6, 1944, Allied troops landed on the beaches of Normandy. Hemingway and Martha were both present. Hemingway was on an observation ship. Gellhorn made it ashore. In August, U.S. forces entered Paris, and Hemingway was present. In September, Allied forces broke through Germany's borders. Both Romania and Bulgaria signed armistices with Allied forces. In 1945, German forces in Italy surrendered, Mussolini was executed in Milan, and Hitler committed suicide. Berlin fell in May. On August 6, America dropped an atomic bomb on the city of Hiroshima, Japan. On August 9, they dropped another atomic bomb on Nagasaki. The Japanese surrendered on September 2, and the war ended. Various sources estimate that between 56 million and 61 million soldiers and civilians died during the war, making it the bloodiest war in human history.

Cuban Revolution

In July 1953, the first action against the existing Cuban government led by Fulgencio Batista took place when rebels attacked the Moncada Barracks in Santiago de Cuba.

Hemingway was a supporter of the Cuban revolution, led by Fidel Castro (*r*). Nevertheless, after the revolution, when the United States cut off relations with the Communist government, Hemingway abandoned his Cuban home and returned to the United States.

The attack was unsuccessful, but it spurred support from those who opposed Batista's rule. Fidel Castro, who participated in the attack, spent two years in prison and was then exiled to Mexico, where he organized a guerrilla army to fight Batista.

In December 1956, a group of eighty-two men, including Castro, landed in Cuba, where they encountered severe resistance from Batista's forces. Those who survived found refuge in the Sierra Maestra Mountains and began to stir support from peasants and students, who resented the suffering caused by Batista's authoritarian rule. The revolutionary forces, led by Castro, his brother Raúl, Che

Guevara, and others, managed to prevail against the larger and better-equipped armies of Batista. In the end, Batista fled to Spain with the millions he had accumulated while the Cuban people starved, and the revolutionaries moved into Havana in 1959 with little resistance.

During the revolution, Hemingway had been worried about the treatment an American author living in Cuba would receive. Hemingway despised Batista and was pro-Castro by default, but he realized the dangers of living in a country whose relationship with the United States was to become greatly strained. Hemingway said,

> I just hope to Christ the United States doesn't cut the sugar quota. That would really tear it. It will make Cuba a gift to the Russians. . . . The anti-United States is building. All Around. Spooks you. If they really turn it on, I'm sure they will put me out of business.

Although the Cuban people continued to revere Hemingway, in July 1959 Hemingway's worry became fact—the United States cut off the sugar quota, setting the stage for a Cuban and Russian alliance. By then, Hemingway and his fourth wife, Mary Welsh, were living in Ketchum, Idaho, his health was rapidly failing, and he was approaching the end of his life.

wouldn't be any good. I'll go if you like. But I Br
dn't live quietly in the country. Not with my own true l
now."
't it rotten? There isn't any use my telling you I love y
know I love you."
s not talk. Talking's all bilge. I'm going away from you,
Michael's coming back."
are you going away?"
ter for you. Better for me." *The Sun Also Rises* "Couldn't w
in the country for a while?" Jake said.

wouldn't be any good. I'll go if you like. But I Br
dn't live quietly in the country. Not with my own true l
now."
't it rotten? There isn't any use my telling you I love y
know I love you."
s not talk. Talking's all bilge. I'm going away from you,
Michael's coming back."
are you going away?"
ter for you. Better for me." *The Sun Also Rises* "Couldn't w
in the country for a while?" Jake said.
wouldn't be any good. I'll go if you like. But I Br
dn't live quietly in the country. Not with my own true l
now."
't it rotten? There isn't any use my telling you I love y
know I love you."
s not talk. Talking's all bilge. I'm going away from you,
Michael's coming back."
are you going away?"
ter for you. Better for me." *The Sun Also Rises*
uldn't we go off in the country for a while?" Jake saic
wouldn't be any good. I'll go if you like. But I Br
dn't live quietly in the country. Not with my own true l
now."
't it rotten? There isn't any use my telling you I love y
know I love you."
s not talk. Talking's all bilge. I'm going away from you,
Michael's coming back."
are you going away?"
ter for you. Better for me." *The Sun Also Rises*
uldn't we go off in the country for a while?" Jake saic
wouldn't be any good. I'll go if you like. But I Br
dn't live quietly in the country. Not with my own true l
now."

Part II: The Writing of Ernest Hemingway

ldn't we go off in the country for a while?" Jake said
wouldn't be any good. I'll go if you like. But I Br
dn't live quietly in the country. Not with my own true l
now."
t it rotten? There isn't any use my telling you I love y
know I love you."
s not talk. Talking's all bilge. I'm going away from you,
Michael's coming back."
are you going away?"
ter for you. Better for me." The Sun Also Rises "Couldn't w
in the country for a while?" Jake said.
wouldn't be any good. I'll go if you like. But I Br
dn't live quietly in the country. Not with my own true l
now."
t it rotten? There isn't any use my telling you I love y
know I love you."
s not talk. Talking's all bilge. I'm going away from you,
Michael's coming back."
are you going away?"
ter for you. Better for me." *The Sun Also Rises* "Couldn't w
in the country for a while?" Jake said.
wouldn't be any good. I'll go if you like. But I Br
dn't live quietly in the country. Not with my own true l
now."
t it rotten? There isn't any use my telling you I love y
know I love you."
s not talk. Talking's all bilge. I'm going away from you,
Michael's coming back."
are you going away?"
ter for you. Better for me." *The Sun Also Rises*
ldn't we go off in the country for a while?" Jake said
wouldn't be any good. I'll go if you like. But I Br
dn't live quietly in the country. Not with my own true l
now."
t it rotten? There isn't any use my telling you I love y
know I love you."
s not talk. Talking's all bilge. I'm going away from you,
Michael's coming back."
are you going away?"
ter for you. Better for me." *The Sun Also Rises*
ldn't we go off in the country for a while?" Jake said
wouldn't be any good. I'll go if you like. But I Br
dn't live quietly in the country. Not with my own true l
now."

Introduction

Hemingway wrote in nearly every genre. He began as a news reporter for the *Kansas City Star* and continued to write for various news organizations throughout his career. He is best known for his fiction—his novels and short stories—but he also wrote poetry, plays, and creative nonfiction about a wide variety of subjects, such as bullfighting, hunting, fishing, and writing. Although he contributed writing to two documentary films on the Spanish Civil War, he generally avoided the genre of the screenplay, leaving the adaptation of his work to other writers, whose writing seldom lived up to his standards.

Hemingway's fiction is often characterized as grim because one of its central themes is the inevitability of death. Yet much of the work's brilliance rests on the way his characters struggle with the realization that all things are mortal and will inevitably die. The violence found in his work is not gratuitous, as some have claimed. It is integral to the realization that death is the final chapter in everyone's story. How we live with that knowledge defines us, just as Hemingway's heroes are defined by how they live with their own mortality. The wound, which is a prevalent theme in his work, is evidence of mortality. For example, consider how critic Philip Young characterizes Robert Jordan, the hero of *For Whom the Bell Tolls*:

> Jordan has learned a lot . . . about how to live and function with his wounds, and he behaves well. He dies, but he has done his job, and the manner of his dying convinced many readers of what his thinking had failed to do: that life is worth living and that there are causes worth dying for.

The refusal to surrender one's "passion for life" in the face of one's inevitable mortality shapes the Hemingway hero. Arthur Waldhorn divides Hemingway's heroes into two categories:

> **The Apprentice:**
> Waldhorn argues that none of Hemingway's apprentices finds any place wholly "good." Their psychic wounds never fully heal and they never entirely master the art of living with them. Despite their efforts at control, they are obliquely passive: life affects them more than they affect it.
>
> **The Exemplar:**
> Waldhorn explains that the exemplar has already suffered and subdued many of the afflictions that still await the apprentice: insomnia and a fear of the dark; passivity and dependence (especially on liquor and sex); superstition and a yearning for religion; and the inability to stop thinking. Skilled, professional, and charismatic, the exemplar is a necessary presence for the apprentice, whose rite of passage must continue.

The types of sports that Hemingway preferred, and those that appear in his fiction, mirror the central theme underscoring his writing. Hunting, fishing, bullfighting, and so on, are sports for which the end is known. They all will end in death. The bullfight is over when the bull dies. The hunt is over when the game has been killed. What matters in these sports is how the sport is executed. What is important is how one conducts oneself while hunting, a point clearly made in the story "The Short, Happy Life of Francis Macomber," or how a matador behaves when confronting a bull in the ring, a quality explained in detail in the novel *The Sun Also Rises*. These sports are symbolic of what Hemingway's fiction shows us about life. Life is a game for which the end is already certain. What matters is how we live in the face of that inevitable end.

The Sun Also Rises made Ernest Hemingway famous when it was published in 1926. The 1957 movie cemented Hemingway's reputation for the next generation.

Chapter 1

The Sun Also Rises

Background on the Writing of *The Sun Also Rises*

Hemingway began writing *The Sun Also Rises* in 1925 just before returning to Paris from a trip to Spain, where he attended the Fiesta de San Fermín in Pamplona with a circle of friends. The first draft was finished by September, one month before the publication of his first major short story collection, *In Our Time*, and two months before he began work on *The Torrents of Spring*.

Despite Hemingway's claim that the novel contained "no autobiography," the book's characters were fashioned after members of his social group and the actions were based largely on "the sequence of events in Hemingway's life in the summer of 1925."

Hemingway wrote the novel in an energetic burst across two months. He was excited about his progress and knew that he had something powerful that would make an impact on the literary world. Indeed he had, for *The Sun Also Rises* became a central novel of the modern literary period, exhibiting a unique style with which most readers of the time were unfamiliar. Linda Wagner-Martin points out that *The Sun Also Rises* was not the novel readers expected it to be. Its style was "so unusual as to be plain troublesome." The style was what modernists such as Ezra Pound were calling for—it was "new."

The Sun Also Rises is a *roman à clef*—a work that disguises real people and events as fictional characters and events. Though it may seem to some to be a romance about

the troubled relationship of Jake Barnes and Brett Ashley, it is, like most modern works, open to various interpretations. Hemingway called *The Sun Also Rises* his most "moral" novel. Hemingway's younger brother, Leicester, said Hemingway's parents, who were devoutly religious, were shocked by the racy content of the novel.
Leicester wrote:

> Our parents, when they finally read *The Sun Also Rises*, were as bewildered and shocked as convent girls visiting a bawdy house. . . . Their emotions were thoroughly shaken and life at home, I remember, was like trying to walk on empty eggshells without cracking any. It was referred to as "that book," in horrified tones.

When *The Sun Also Rises* was published in 1926, it became the hallmark work describing expatriates in Europe, an ideal chronicle of the Lost Generation. It helped launch Hemingway as a major modern novelist. Wagner-Martin summed up the novel's significance well when she wrote,

> Most writers' first novels do not turn out to be their most important work. In Ernest Hemingway's case, *The Sun Also Rises* has gradually come to have just that reputation. . . . Hemingway wrote his 1926 novel with a sense of surety, a knowledge of craft, and a belief that literature could create morality. He produced a document of the chaotic postwar 1920s and a testament to the writer's ability to create characters, mood, situation, and happenings that were as real as life.

The Sun Also Rises transformed Hemingway from a promising young author into a major literary figure.

Much of its success rests on Hemingway's ability to capture many of the artistic goals of the time. The novel's prose style is terse and reverberates with a sense of loss and despair. The subject matter, which covers Spanish bullfights, infidelity, marriages of convenience, careless living, homosexuality, anti-Semitism, post-war depression, and characters who reject conventional society, was unusual for the time and represented a break from the subject matter of traditional novels. Perhaps most significantly, the novel exposes a unique authorial imagination that successfully reveals the psychological lives of the novel's characters through a precise rendering of crisp physical detail.

The Principal Characters in *The Sun Also Rises*

Jacob "Jake" Barnes

Jake Barnes narrates the story, and everything that he tells us is colored by his perceptions, making it unlikely that everything he is telling us is trustworthy. He is an American expatriate living on the Left Bank in Paris and working as a journalist for a news service. Jake is impotent from a wound he received in World War I, which prevents him from pursuing a lasting relationship with Brett Ashley, the woman he desires. Jake is fond of fishing and is an *aficionado* (someone who is passionate about a sport) of bullfighting. Every year he attends the running of the bulls in Spain. He spends his time drinking, socializing, commenting on his acquaintances, and struggling to make sense of his life, which has seemingly been rendered aimless by his wound.

Despite his flaws (e.g., his anti-Semitic attitudes), Jake is a sympathetic character. He struggles to find meaning in a world rendered absurd by war, but his wound has made it impossible for him to fashion a meaningful life for himself. Nevertheless, he refuses to surrender completely to despair, and so remains balanced above the abyss the war left behind. He has no reason to hope that he can realize a life with Brett, yet he continues to stand against the inevitable. His persistence in the face of overwhelming odds mirrors the bullring, wherein the bullfighter stands his ground against a charging bull. As he tells Cohn in Chapter 2, "Nobody ever lives their life all the way up except bull-fighters" (p. 10).

The character of Jake Barnes is loosely based on Ernest Hemingway. (Although Hemingway was wounded, he was not impotent.)

Robert Cohn

Robert Cohn is a thirty-four-year-old Jewish-American expatriate who, like Jake, lives in Paris. Cohn graduated from Princeton, where he was middleweight boxing champion. Cohn is portrayed as a pathetic character. He is dominated by the women in his life and lacks confidence. He came from a well-to-do New York family, but blew most of his money.

At the opening of the novel, Cohn is romantically linked with Frances Clyne, who grew disgusted with Cohn in America and talked him into moving to Europe so she could "get what there was to get while there was still something available" (p. 5). Jake is Cohn's "tennis friend." Like Jake, Cohn falls for Brett Ashley, with whom he has a short fling.

Cohn is an object of ridicule throughout the novel, and is at odds with most of the other characters. Jake, at best, tolerates Cohn and often makes reference to the fact that Cohn is a Jew. One instance occurs at the beginning of the novel when Jake makes "anti-Semitic wisecracks, which include a dissertation on how Cohn's Jewish nose was 'certainly improved' by being flattened in a boxing match at Princeton." Jake never saw Cohn's nose prior to it being altered; thus, his implied condemnation of

Cohn's original nose betrays an anti-Semitic viewpoint. Despite these jabs at Cohn, some critics, such as scholar James Nagel, argue that Jake and Cohn are, at the beginning of the novel, "quite good friends, unencumbered by what some readers have come to regard as Jake's anti-Semitism."

Cohn possesses many qualities that Jake would presumably admire. He is a strong fighter, yet he exhibits restraint when he is confronted; he is a successful novelist, a goal to which Jake aspires; and he shares Jake's love for Brett. But Jake, like many of Hemingway's characters, is more concerned with *how* people behave than with the outcomes of those behaviors, and Cohn's behavior (his inability to adhere to the appropriate code of living) is the object of much derision throughout the novel.

The character of Robert Cohn is based on Harold Loeb. Loeb was a writer who attended Princeton and attended the fiesta in Pamplona in 1925. Loeb had an affair with Lady Duff Twysden (the model for Brett Ashley), to whom Hemingway was also attracted.

Lady Brett Ashley

Brett Ashley is the focal point around whom much of the action of the novel occurs. She is a "liberated" Englishwoman of the 1920s. She drinks, smokes, and engages in multiple flings with men. Brett is a strong woman. She dominates the men she encounters and has no reservations about taking charge of her own life, going where she wants, when she wants, and with whom she wants. Nevertheless, a sense of directionless ambiguity surrounds her.

During the war, she met and fell in love with Jake while he was in the hospital recovering from wounds suffered on the battlefront. Despite her feelings for Jake, she married Lord Ashley. At the time of the novel, she is divorcing Lord Ashley and is engaged to Mike Campbell, a bankrupt drunkard, who is expecting a large inheritance one day. Brett is a complex character who is both dependent on the men around her (primarily for financial support) and insistent on her independence from their rule.

Brett's character reflects the changing role of women in America during the 1920s. Like Jake, Brett is struggling to find her place in the world and is disillusioned and searching for satisfaction in her life. The love she shares with Jake drives the central conflict in the novel, for Jake's wound makes it impossible for this love to be fully realized.

Like many of the characters in *The Sun Also Rises*, Brett is a study in contradictions: She is sexually liberated and independent, while remaining financially and psychologically dependent on the men in her life. Wendy Martin argues that "Brett's loose, disordered relationships reflect the shattered unity and contradictions of the modern world."

The character of Brett Ashley is based on Lady Duff Twysden (who was born Dorothy Smurthwaite), an attractive socialite to whom Hemingway took a fancy. According to Alice Hunt Sokoloff, Hadley, Hemingway's first wife, considered Duff "wonderfully attractive, a real woman of the world with no sexual inhibitions." During the Pamplona trip, which Duff attended with her lover Pat Guthrie (the model for Mike Campbell), Duff had affairs with Harold Loeb (the model for Robert Cohn) and, at Hemingway's prompting, bullfighter Cayetano Ordoñez (the model for Pedro Romero).

Mike Campbell

Mike Campbell is an anti-Semitic Scottish businessman who has gone bankrupt through dealings with unscrupulous partners. He is engaged to Brett Ashley. He claims to tolerate her affairs with other men, but occasionally becomes jealous, and absorbs her insults without flinching. Mike handles money poorly and often has to rely on others to pay his way. Like many of the characters in the book, he is an alcoholic. Despite his poor handling of financial matters, he comes from a wealthy family. He is jovial and easygoing, except when incensed by Cohn, and accepts life as it comes, without judgment. But unlike Pedro, he is graceless.

> *The character of Mike Campbell is based on Pat Guthrie. Guthrie was engaged to Lady Duff Twysden. He was Scottish, short on funds, and "fond of the vine."*

Pedro Romero

Pedro Romero is a nineteen-year-old bullfighter. Attractive and dignified, Romero catches the interest of Jake and Brett. He is heroic, brave, masculine, in control of his destiny, and the only man in the novel who is not submissive to Brett.

Pedro is contrasted with the other men in the novel. From Jake's point of view, Pedro is the ideal man. He faces the bull in the arena without fear and carries himself well. He is an example of a Hemingway code hero, matching the description Philip Young offers for bullfighters:

> The bullfighter is a good example of the man with the code. As he acts out his role as high priest of a ceremonial in which men pit themselves against violent death, and, with a behavior that formalizes the code, administers what men seek to avoid, he is the very personification of "grace under pressure."

Pedro is also sexually vital. He is the man Jake wishes he were. Pedro does not back down from the bulls, and he does not back down from Cohn, who is the stronger fighter, when they battle over Brett.

Pedro is introduced to Brett by Jake, and so becomes a surrogate for Jake, interacting with Brett in a way that is impossible for Jake. Through Pedro we learn those qualities of manhood that Jake considers important and those manly qualities to which Brett is attracted.

The character of Pedro Romero is based on bullfighter Cayetano Ordoñez. Pedro Romero is named for one of the most important figures in bullfighting, an eighteenth-century matador who killed more than 5,600 bulls without a single injury to himself. Ordoñez was born in 1904 and is credited with resurrecting the art of bullfighting.

Bill Gorton

Bill Gorton is an American writer on vacation. A rapacious drinker, he provides humor in the novel. Bill is Jake's friend. He is also attracted to Brett Ashley, but does not pursue her because she is married.

Bill provides Jake with a link to the natural world, and Jake is most content when he and Bill are fishing. Bill is Jake's confidante, the one to whom he confesses his love for Brett. He also voices the exchange of values that runs thematically through the novel. When he and Jake pass a Parisian taxidermist's shop, Bill, who wants Jake to buy a stuffed dog, says to Jake, "Mean everything in the world to you after you bought it. Simple exchange of values. You give them the money. They give you a stuffed dog" (p. 72). Although Bill is comically drunk when he offers Jake this insight, the statement resonates throughout the novel, and we find Jake wrestling with how the balance between what is given and what is received is measured. This is apparent when Jake, agonizing over Brett, offers as his philosophy that he "had been having Brett for a friend . . . [and] had not been thinking about her side of it. . . . [He] had been getting something for nothing . . . [but] the bill always came. . . . Just exchange of values" (p. 148).

Jake's philosophical determination that life is an "exchange of values" offers him a way to live in the world. It is his way of imposing meaning on a world that resists meaning. Though the philosophy may be seen by some as flawed, it is, as Waldhorn notes, a means for Jake to "escape the stagnation afflicting most of his fellows."

The character of Bill Gorton is based on a mixture of William "Bill" Smith and Donald Ogden Stewart. Stewart was a successful American humorist who became an important screenwriter. Some of his screenplays include An Affair to Remember *(1957),* The Prisoner of Zenda *(1937), and* The Philadelphia Story *(1940), for which he won an Academy Award. Smith and Hemingway had been friends since childhood.*

Count Mippipopolous

Count Mippipopolous is a fat, wealthy Greek count. The count is free with his money. He is introduced to Brett by a portrait painter named Zizi.

Mippipopolous provides important insight into Brett's character. He offers Brett ten thousand dollars to accompany him to Biarritz. Although she likes him, she refuses, which shows that her financial dependence on men does not completely control her decisions. The fact that she tells Jake soon after the offer further suggests that her feelings for Jake are sincere.

Mippipopolous provides a contrast to Jake. Like Jake, he is a veteran and was wounded in the war. He has fought in seven wars and four revolutions. Unlike Jake, Mippipopolous is proud of his wounds. Just as the bullfighter Pedro Romero represents the ideal man to Jake, Mippipopolous represents the practical man. Mippipopolous is at peace in the world. As he explains to Jake, "You see, Mr. Barnes, it is because I have lived very much that now I can enjoy everything so well. . . . That is the secret. You must get to know the values" (p. 60). Mippipopolous is an example of the type of character Waldhorn calls an "exemplar." He has achieved what Jake seeks—a way of living in a world.

Frances Clyne

Frances Clyne is Robert Cohn's fiancée. She dominates him and was the one who talked him into traveling to Europe so he could write. Frances becomes angry and vindictive when Cohn breaks off their relationship.

Like Brett, Frances is financially dependent on men, inviting comparison between the two women. However, Frances lacks Brett's free-spirited independence. Brett's interest in Cohn is based on pity. Frances's interest in Cohn is based on financial necessity. Frances has few other options. Her mother lost the family's resources in bad investments, and Frances walked away from her previous husband (and alimony) in order to better her situation with Cohn. As Brett represents the increased liberation of women in the modern age, Frances represents the dangers of clinging to the heritage of the past.

The character of Frances Clyne is based on Kathleen "Kitty" Cannell. Kitty was involved with Harold Loeb before Loeb's affair with Duff Twysden. Hemingway first met his second wife, Pauline, at a party thrown by Loeb and Kitty in March 1925.

Overview of *The Sun Also Rises*

Book I

The Sun Also Rises is divided into three sections (Book I, Book II, and Book III) and begins with the sentence, "Robert Cohn was once middleweight boxing champion of Princeton" (p. 3). Originally, Hemingway had begun with the claim, "This is a novel about a lady. Her name is Lady Ashley and when the story begins, she is living in Paris and it is Spring." Following the advice of F. Scott Fitzgerald, Hemingway made substantial cuts and revisions to the opening before publication, claiming that the book would "move much faster from the start that way." (Later in life, he would deny Fitzgerald's influence on his work.) The novel is narrated by Jake Barnes.

Chapter 1

In Chapter 1, Jake introduces Robert Cohn. Cohn is a former boxer, a Princeton graduate, and an author. His father is from "one of the richest Jewish families in New York" and his mother is from "one of the oldest" (p. 4). The fact that Cohn is Jewish is significant. In the 1920s, when Hemingway was writing *The Sun Also Rises*, anti-Semitism was widely prevalent in America. Hemingway scholar Michael Reynolds points out that a "virulent strain of anti-Semitism . . . broke out in America after the Great War [World War I]," and that the "American scene was filled with fears and prejudices, all in the name of nationalism." Cohn is the novel's target for much of that sentiment.

> I mistrust all frank and simple people, especially when their stories hold together.
> Jake Barnes, *The Sun Also Rises*, p. 4

Cohn, who is dominated by the women in his life, married the "first girl who was nice to him" (p. 4). During the five years of his marriage, he and his wife had three children. After she left him for an artist, he moved to California, where he entered literary circles. There he became involved with Frances Clyne, who urges him to go to Europe. Jake recounts a time when he suggested, in front of Frances, that he and Cohn go to Strasbourg where he knows a girl who can show them around. Cohn kicks Jake under the table to quiet him, and Jake realizes the control Frances has over Cohn's movements. According to Jake, Cohn only has two friends: Braddock, who is his "literary friend," and Jake, who is his "tennis friend" (p. 5).

Jake's appraisal of Cohn is negative and belittling, which sets Cohn in opposition to the narrator and summons a number of comparisons throughout the novel. Both Jake and Cohn claim to love Brett, both are impotent (Jake by way of his war wound and Cohn by way of his ineffectual personality), both are unrequited lovers who are unable to prolong their relationship with Brett, both are at the mercy of her whims, and both are writers living abroad.

The narrative stance introduced in the first chapter colors the rest of the novel. Jake is telling the story after all the events have taken place and his current attitudes about the other characters influence his descriptions of past events. Although readers are not yet aware of what is to happen, Jake's ridicule of Cohn, which we first see in Chapter 1 and which runs throughout the novel, reflects Jake's opinion of Cohn after their friendship has ended.

Chapter 2

Chapter 2 moves the story of Cohn forward one year. Cohn's novel had been accepted for publication and, on a related trip to New York, Cohn realizes that women have begun to take more interest in him. He appears vainer than before, and worries that life is quickly passing him by. Inspired by W. H. Hudson's *The Purple Land*, he wants to travel to South America, believing that a foreign land will add adventure to his life. He invites Jake to accompany him. Jake declines, explaining that "going to another country doesn't make any difference" (p. 11). The two go to Jake's office, where Jake works for two hours while Cohn is lulled to sleep by the sound of the typewriter. When Jake wakes him, Cohn spouts out, "I can't do it" (p. 12). Jake and Cohn visit Café Napolitain for an aperitif (cocktail).

> Nobody ever lives their life all the way up except bull-fighters.
> Jake Barnes, *The Sun Also Rises*, p. 10

A key difference between Cohn and Jake is established in Chapter 2. The ease with which Cohn is influenced by the work of W. H. Hudson, a writer of South American romances, exposes his tendency to romanticize the world. Cohn is unable to accept the world as it is, and imagines that a trip to South America will offer him the excitement and personal satisfaction he seeks. But Jake is under no such delusion. He has a more practical view of the world. He realizes that the "splendid imaginary amorous adventures of a perfect English gentleman in an intensely romantic land" that Hudson writes about are unrealistic fantasies (p. 9). When Cohn invites Jake to visit South America with him, Jake refuses, realizing that Cohn is on a fool's quest. Jake says, "I've tried all that. You can't get away from yourself by moving from one place to another. There's nothing to that" (p. 11).

Key to this difference between Jake and Cohn is fear. Despite his interest in experiencing life, Cohn is unwilling to embark alone on a trip to South America. Jake, as we discover throughout the novel, is not afraid to experience life; thus, Cohn seeks to borrow Jake's strength in order to pursue a more meaningful life.

Both attitudes will play out in how each man handles his relationship with Brett in later chapters, as Jake reconciles himself to the impossibility of consummating his love, and Cohn refuses to accept Brett's dismissal of him.

Chapter 3

After Cohn has left the café, Jake meets a prostitute named Georgette and invites her to dinner. In the cab on the way to the restaurant, she makes an advance, touching him suggestively. He pulls her hand away, explaining that he is "sick." Later, she asks again about what is wrong with him, and he explains that he was injured in the war.

> She [Georgette] cuddled against me [Jake] and I put my arm around her. She looked to be kissed. She touched me with one hand and I put her hand away.
> "Never mind."
> "What's the matter? You sick?"
> "Yes."
> *The Sun Also Rises*, p. 15

At the restaurant, Jake and Georgette encounter two other couples (Mr. and Mrs. Braddocks and Cohn and Frances) and join their party. Jake jokingly introduces Georgette as his fiancé, a jest that the dimwitted Mrs. Braddocks fails to get. After dinner, they all go to a dancing club where they run into Brett Ashley with a group of homosexual men. Jake becomes angry and retreats to a bar next door for a drink. His anger, though motivated by jealousy, is related to his frustration at not being able to form a relationship with Brett because of his wound. The unspoken question his anger implies is: If Brett can form bonds with homosexual men without the promise of physical love, why can't she form a bond with Jake? Also at issue is a central question of the novel: What does it mean to be a man? When Jake returns from the bar,

Georgette is dancing with one of the homosexual men, paralleling Brett's earlier actions. This time, Jake does not react, which highlights the difference between Georgette and Brett and implies that more was involved in Jake's anger than he claimed when he said that it was the homosexual men who "always made . . . [him] angry" (p. 20).

Mrs. Braddocks introduces Jake to a rising novelist named Robert Prentiss and Jake and Prentiss get a drink at the bar, where Brett joins them. Cohn approaches and asks Brett to dance. She declines. Jake leaves fifty francs for Georgette and Jake and Brett leave together. In the cab, Brett tells Jake that she has been miserable.

Throughout Chapter 3, without explicitly stating it, Hemingway reveals that Jake is harboring deep feelings for Brett, and that Brett, at least partly, shares those feelings.

Chapter 4

The feelings implied at the end of Chapter 3 become explicit in Chapter 4. Jake and Brett kiss while driving around Paris, and the suspicion that they are in love is confirmed, but Brett pulls back from Jake. They visit the Café Select, where they once again run into their friends. Zizi, a painter, introduces them to his patron, Count Mippipopolous. Jake makes plans to meet Brett the next day, and returns home alone where he reads the bullfighting papers.

> Probably I never would have had any trouble if I hadn't run into Brett when they shipped me to England. I suppose she only wanted what she couldn't have. Well, people were that way. To hell with people.
> Jake Barnes, *The Sun Also Rises*, p. 31

At 4:30 in the morning, Brett shows up and, after making a scene with the concierge, goes to Jake's room. She tells him that Mippipopolous offered her ten thousand dollars to accompany him to Biarritz, but she refused. The count is downstairs waiting to take them to a champagne breakfast. She wants Jake to come with them, but he says no. After she leaves, he falls into despair, saying "It is awfully easy to be hard-boiled about everything in the daytime, but at night it is another thing" (p. 34).

Chapter 4 outlines Brett's affection for Jake and their past relationship. We discover that both Jake and Brett are emotionally distraught over the impossibility of a lasting relationship, which heightens the tension between the two characters. The chapter also introduces Count Mippipopolous, who operates as the novel's voice of reason.

Chapter 5

Jake spends the morning working. At around 11:00 AM, he takes a cab to a press conference at the Quai d'Orsay, where he listens to a French diplomat field questions. Afterward he shares a cab with two other reporters. Cohn is waiting for him in his office when he returns. At lunch, Cohn confesses that he has fallen for Brett, and he pumps Jake for information about her.

Chapter 5 establishes the depth of Cohn's attraction to Brett, further illustrating the contrast between the two men that was established in Chapters 1 and 2. Cohn's dialogue with Jake is romanticized and a bit naïve, while Jake's dialogue remains tempered and matter-of-fact. For example, Cohn claims that Brett is "a remarkably attractive woman . . . absolutely fine and straight." Though he does not contradict Cohn, Jake admits only that Brett is "very nice" (p. 38). Cohn doesn't believe Brett would "marry anybody she didn't love" (p. 39), while Jake, who sticks to "the facts" (p. 38), informs Cohn that she has "done it twice" already, which Cohn refuses to believe (p. 39). This exchange is important to our understanding of Jake. Jake is not, like Cohn, deluded by romantic notions.

He sees Brett for who she is and loves her, whereas Cohn imagines her to be the type of woman he wants to love.

> "She's [Brett] a drunk," I [Jake] said. "She's in love with Mike Campbell and she's going to marry him. He's going to be rich as hell some day."
> "I [Cohn] don't believe she'll ever marry him."
> "Why not?"
> "I don't know. I just don't believe it."
> *The Sun Also Rises*, p. 38

Chapter 5 also heightens the complexity of Brett's character. We learn that she is married to one man, whom she plans to divorce, while she is engaged to another—Mike Campbell. These revelations, which would have shocked many readers in 1926, do not lessen Cohn's interest in Brett.

Chapter 6

Brett fails to show up for her date with Jake, further revealing conflict in their relationship. Jake takes a taxi to the Café Select where he runs into Harvey Stone, a friend who is down on his luck and on a drinking binge. Jake lends him one hundred francs. Cohn shows up and Stone leaves after tossing several insults at Cohn, further illustrating the general contempt that people feel for Cohn.

Cohn admits to Jake that he is having difficulty starting his next novel. When his fiancée, Frances, arrives, we realize how much Cohn is dominated by her. She treats Cohn harshly. At one point, she pulls Jake off for a private conversation and we learn the source of much of her animosity—Cohn is refusing to marry her. When Jake and Frances rejoin Cohn, Frances ridicules him about his plan to send her away to England.

> "Here comes Cohn," I [Jake] said. Robert Cohn was crossing the street.
> "That moron," said Harvey. Cohn came up to our table.
> "Hello, you bums," he said.
> "Hello, Robert," Harvey said. "I was just telling Jake here that you're a moron."
> *The Sun Also Rises*, p. 43.

Cohn's reactions to Stone's insults early in the chapter invite a contrast to the way he handles Frances's insults. When Stone calls Cohn a moron, Cohn confronts him. When Stone refuses to back off, Cohn tells him that "some day somebody will push your face in" (p. 44). However, when Frances, a woman, insults him, Cohn fails to stand up to her. Jake is shocked by Cohn's weakness around a woman. Disgusted, he makes an orchestrated exit.

Chapter 7

Jake returns home from his encounter with Cohn and Frances, and the concierge tells him that a lady (Brett) and a gentleman (Count Mippipopolous) had stopped by. She also gives him a telegram from his friend Bill Gorton, who is planning a trip to Paris.

Brett and the count return to find Jake despondent. Jake asks her why she missed their date; she claims to have forgotten. The count points out that she was drunk. However, readers are left with the sense that complex emotions are at work beneath Brett's casual explanation.

While the count is out of the room, finding a vase for the roses he has brought, Brett asks Jake, who is obviously out of sorts, what is troubling him, and he confesses his love for her. Recognizing the seriousness of Jake's emotional state, Brett sends the count out to buy champagne, so that she and Jake can be alone.

"Couldn't we go off in the country for a while?" [Jake said.]
"It wouldn't be any good. I'll go if you like. But I [Brett] couldn't live quietly in the country. Not with my own true love."
"I know."
"Isn't it rotten? There isn't any use my telling you I love you."
"You know I love you."
"Let's not talk. Talking's all bilge. I'm going away from you, and then Michael's coming back."
"Why are you going away?"
"Better for you. Better for me."
The Sun Also Rises, p. 55

In the brief conversation that follows, Jake questions her about the possibility of them being together. Realizing that a relationship with Jake would be doomed to failure, and admitting that she would inevitably deceive him "with everybody," Brett dismisses his suggestion that they get together, but not before confessing that she loves him (p. 55). Brett's tone remains casual, but the exchange raises the question of whether or not Brett is rejecting Jake because she loves him and knows that if they were together, she would make a mess of his life. She says, "It's my fault, Jake. It's the way I'm made" (p. 55).

Jake also learns that Brett has already made plans to make a trip to San Sebastian, in Spain, with Cohn. When the count returns with the champagne, the mood in the room is tense. Jake, Brett, and the count drink three bottles while the count talks about his experiences. He has been in "seven wars and four revolutions" and shows them his scars (p. 60). The Count is an important voice in the novel, and from him we learn that wisdom is gained through experience, a frequent Hemingway theme. The Count's ability to take life as it comes parallels Jake's acceptance of his condition, and the men find common ground in their mutual preference for "quiet." Brett, in contrast, prefers "noise" (p. 61). The three of them go to dinner and a nightclub. Afterward, Jake takes Brett home, but she refuses to let him come in, telling him that she won't see him again, thus ending Book I with Jake's inability to regain the love he has lost.

Book II

Chapter 8

Book II begins after Cohn and Brett's trip to San Sebastian, thereby skipping Cohn and Brett's romantic encounter and further emphasizing Jake's point of view. Like Jake, readers do not witness any tenderness between Cohn and Brett, only the bitter aftermath.

> We [Jake and Bill] walked on and circled the island. The river was dark and a bateau mouche [speedboat] went by, all bright with lights, going fast and quiet up and out of sight under the bridge. Down the river was Notre Dame squatting against the night sky. We crossed to the left bank of the Seine by the wooden foot-bridge from the Quai de Bethune, and stopped on the bridge and looked down the river at Notre Dame. Standing on the bridge the island looked dark, the houses were high against the sky, and the tresses were shadows.
>
> Jake Barnes, *The Sun Also Rises*, p. 77

Chapter 8 is a preamble to the fishing trip that takes place in the next chapter. Bill Gorton has arrived in Paris after spending three weeks visiting Budapest and Vienna. Bill, like many characters in the novel, drinks heavily and struggles to recall for Jake events that occurred during a four-day binge in Vienna.

Jake and Bill have drinks and then head out for dinner, stopping for more drinks several times along the way. Before they get to the restaurant, they run into Brett, who tells them that her fiancé, Mike Campbell, is expected that evening. This is the first time Jake has seen Brett since she returned from her trip with Cohn. She joins the two men for drinks, and, after arranging to meet up with them later, excuses herself to go get ready for Mike's arrival.

Jake and Bill dine at Madame Lecomte's, a restaurant jammed with Americans seeking an authentic French dining experience. The presence of these "compatriots" bothers Jake (p. 76). They echo the romantic sentiment attributed to Cohn in the first two chapters of the novel. Like Cohn, they desire the romantic experiences offered by other countries; yet, rather than blending with the cultures they visit, they overrun them.

After dinner, Jake and Bill browse the city, finally arriving at the Café Select, where they meet up with Brett and Mike. Mike is drunk and anxious to spend time alone with Brett. The chapter ends with Jake and Bill agreeing to take in a boxing match.

Chapter 9

Cohn reenters the narrative in Chapter 9, and the story shifts away from Paris. Jake has received a letter from Cohn saying he is looking forward to accompanying Jake and Bill on their fishing trip. Jake writes him back saying that he and Bill will be leaving on the 25th. That evening, Jake heads to the Café Select to visit with Brett and Mike. Mike invites himself and Brett on the fishing trip. Because Cohn, whom Brett is now trying to avoid, will be on the trip, the stage is set for trouble. Jake hopes that Cohn will back out once he knows that Mike and Brett will also be present.

On the 25th, Jake and Bill take the train from Gare d'Orsay. They meet an American family on the train. The husband and wife bicker about the husband's drinking, prompting the wife to remark, "It's a wonder they [men] ever find any one to marry them" (p. 86). This further accentuates the differences between men and women, which are highlighted throughout the novel. The husband mentions that there are "plenty of Americans" on the train (p. 85). Their presence echoes the "compatriots" whom Jake and Bill encountered at the restaurant in the previous chapter. They too have traveled to Europe under the notion that foreign lands will add spice to their lives, yet they are disillusioned, a point highlighted by their frequent jabs at each other.

> Brett looked at me. "I say," she said, "is Robert Cohn going on this trip?"
> "Yes. Why?" I said.
> "Don't you think it will be a bit rough on him?"
> "Why should it?"
> "Who did you think I went down to San Sebastian with?"
> "Congratulations," I said.
> We walked along.
> "What did you say that for?"
> "I don't know. What would you like me to say?"
> *The Sun Also Rises*, p. 83.

The infusion of Americans into the European landscape contributes to the foreboding sense of loss that underscores the novel. Europe is changing in the wake of World War I, and American interest in the continent threatens to erase the authentic experience that Europe once offered. Jake is particularly disturbed by the intrusion of Americans into his experience. Americans are forcing themselves onto European culture. Jake's life has been transformed by the war on an individual level just as the nature of the world has been transformed on a global level.

At the close of Chapter 9, when Jake and Bill's train arrives in Bayonne, France, Cohn is waiting for them.

Chapter 10

Jake, Bill, and Cohn are in Bayonne preparing to start their fishing trip the next day. Brett and Mike are supposed to arrive that evening. Bill bets Cohn that they will arrive on time, but Bill loses the bet when Jake receives a telegram from Brett and Mike saying they have been held up in San Sebastian.

We discover during the course of the chapter that Jake is jealous of Cohn's previous trip to San Sebastian with Brett and that Cohn had arranged a date with Brett in San Sebastian, which explains why she delayed leaving for Bayonne. Jake and Bill plan to take the bus to Burguete in the morning, but Cohn decides to stay behind to wait for Brett and Mike.

> After a while we [Jake, Bill, and Cohn] came out of the mountain, and there were trees along both sides of the road, and a stream and ripe fields of grain, and the road went on, very white and straight ahead, and then lifted to a little rise, and off on the left was a hill with an old castle, with buildings close around it and a field of grain going right up to the walls and shifting in the wind.
> Jake Barnes, *The Sun Also Rises*, p. 93

In Chapter 10, Cohn's misreading of his encounter with Brett is exposed. Blinded by romantic delusions, Cohn is portrayed as pathetic in his mooning for her. Jake and Bill are annoyed by Cohn's behavior. Jake admits that his annoyance is prompted by his jealousy over Cohn's encounter with Brett:

> Why I felt that impulse to devil him [Cohn] I do not know. Of course I do know. I was blind, unforgivingly jealous of what had happened to him. The fact that I took it as a matter of course did not alter that any. I certainly did hate him (p. 99).

It is clear from Cohn's interactions with others that he is socially awkward and does not know how to fit in, but, under the misguided belief that he has something with Brett that Mike and Jake do not have, he continues to impose his presence where it is not wanted.

Chapter 11

Jake and Bill ride the bus through the scenic Basque landscape to Burguete. Along the way they converse with the other passengers and share wine. In Burguete they rent a room at an inn.

The bus ride in Chapter 11 contrasts with the train ride in Chapter 9. Unlike the train, the bus is full of native Europeans, friendly Basques who welcome Jake and Bill's company. The scenery is pleasant and Jake and Bill have an enjoyable trip and an authentic European experience.

> He [an old Basque man] shook hands and turned around to the back seat again. . . . He sat back comfortably and smiled at me when I turned around to look at the country. But the effort of talking American seemed to have tired him. He did not say anything after that.
> Jake Barnes, *The Sun Also Rises*, p. 108

They talk with an old Basque man who had visited America forty years earlier. This inverts what we found in Chapter 9: Jake and Bill encountered Americans visiting Europe; now, they encounter a European who has visited America. When they buy the man a drink, he says, "You can't get this in America, eh?" [because of Prohibition](p. 107). The comment encompasses more than just the wine, implying that the unique experience offered by Europe is unavailable in America, thus highlighting our understanding of what is at risk when Americans, full of romantic notions, flood into Europe.

Chapter 12

Jake wakes up early and goes outside to dig worms while Bill sleeps. Over breakfast, Bill calls Jake an expatriate:

> You're an expatriate. You've lost touch with the soil. You get precious. Fake European standards have ruined you. You drink yourself to death. You become obsessed by sex. You spend all your time talking, not working. You are an expatriate, see? You hang around cafés. . . . You don't work. (p. 115)

The subject of Jake's wound is raised and quickly dropped.

The two men fish separately and then meet for lunch. At the end of the chapter, we are told that they fished for five days without hearing from Cohn, Brett, or Mike.

Chapter 12 introduces two ideas. First, the notion that nature is restorative. Jake and Bill's fishing trip is a peaceful period following the emotional tension of the first ten chapters. The outdoors, which Hemingway relished and wrote about throughout his life, is a place of solace and comfort.

Second, Hemingway portrays in this section his view of male bonding. In the absence of civilization, intrusive American tourists, women, and the complications sexual relationships create, Jake and Bill are able to relax in each other's company and, most importantly, accept one another. Bill considers Jake no less a man because of Jake's wound. The fishing trip contrasts the life in "cafés" that Bill attributes to expatriates; it is Jake's moment to reconnect to "the soil" (p. 115).

Chapters 11 and 12 set up an important contrast between the easy camaraderie that is possible among men and the difficult and often confusing relationships between men and women. Jake, like many of Hemingway's heroes, finds a type of comfort in the company of men that is unavailable with women.

Chapter 13

After nearly a week of fishing, Jake receives a telegram from Mike apologizing for being late and saying that he and Brett are now at the Hotel Montoya in Pamplona. Before taking the bus to Pamplona to meet up with the rest of their group, Jake and Bill share several bottles of wine with the Englishman, Harris.

In Pamplona, Jake and Bill take rooms at the Hotel Montoya, where the good bullfighters stay. Montoya, who runs the hotel, is impressed by Jake's understanding of bullfighting and refers to him as an aficionado.

> Why don't you ever get drunk, Robert? You know you didn't have a good time at San Sebastian because none of our friends would invite you on any of the parties.
> Mike Campbell, *The Sun Also Rises,* p. 142

The group attends the *desencajonada* (the releasing of the bulls into the corral) where steers are used to quiet the bulls and are often killed. When a steer is gored, Cohn remarks, "It's no life being a steer" (p. 141). Mike compares Cohn to a steer following Brett around. During the argument that follows, we learn that Cohn's nickname for Brett is "Circe," a Greek goddess who could turn men into swine. Later, the mood calms and they all have dinner.

Chapter 13 marks the middle of the novel and introduces readers to the bullfighting. The descriptions of bullfighting found in *The Sun Also Rises* are some of the first to appear in American literature. They also serve many symbolic purposes for the novel. The ring, which symbolizes life, is where a bullfighter faces a bull, an act that parallels a man facing danger, like a soldier in war. Hemingway contends that life is richer and more meaningful when danger is involved, and that a man is manlier when he faces this danger without flinching.

BULLFIGHTING WAS AN ESSENTIAL ELEMENT OF THE TENSION IN HEMINGWAY'S FIRST NOVEL.

Significant, too, is the mention of steers (castrated bulls). Jake is physically like a castrated bull, though his wound is never explicitly described, and Mike pointedly calls Cohn a steer, which Cohn resents. This raises the question: What makes a man less of a man—physical or psychological impotence? Is Jake less of a man because he can no longer have physical relations with Brett, or is Cohn less of a man because of his weak and ineffectual nature?

The symbolic use of bullfights to illuminate manhood continues through the end of Book II.

Chapter 14

Jake goes to bed, but cannot sleep because his head is spinning from too much alcohol. He hears Cohn and Brett in the hallway and then hears Brett and Mike in the next room. He reads and muses about how his relationship with Brett has been uneven—he has gotten something for nothing and now the bill has come and he must pay. As Jake sees it, he has received companionship and affection from Brett, but is unable to fulfill her need for physical love. Thus he must suffer, by seeing her with other men, in order to repay his debt to her—which he understatedly refers to as a simple "exchange of values" (p. 148).

> I could not sleep. There is no reason why because it is dark you should look at things differently from when it is light. The hell there isn't.
>
> I figured that all out once, and for six months I never slept with the electric light off. That was another bright idea. To hell with women, anyway. To hell with you, Brett Ashley.
> Jake Barnes, *The Sun Also Rises*, p. 148

Jake is searching for a way to exist in a world that resists understanding. Philosophy and religion fail to offer adequate guidance. In their absence, he speculates that

"Maybe if you found out how to live in it you learned from that what it was all about" (p. 148). The ability to live in the world is an important part of the Hemingway code. Jake's retreat to his room in Chapter 14 "lets him release his subjective feelings through an interior monologue." The "unforgettable passages of introspection" found in this chapter, as Waldhorn notes, "provide a necessary, humanizing glimpse into the heart of his darkness (where also resides the thematic center of the novel) and accent his awesome task of adjustment."

The remainder of the chapter recounts how the days pass quietly as the town prepares for the running of the bulls. Brett and Jake visit a church, Cohn follows and the three have a surprisingly pleasant afternoon.

Chapter 15

Jake describes the start of the fiesta, which opens with fireworks. The streets are filled with observers, dancers, musicians, and an assortment of odd characters. At one point, dancers surround Brett, making her the center of their attention. This mirrors the central role she plays among her social circle (particularly the men). Jake buys a couple of wine skins. Cohn passes out from too much drinking too early in the morning and sleeps for two hours atop wine casks. That evening, after a large meal, Jake tries to stay up to watch the running of the bulls at 6:00 AM, but falls asleep at 4:00 AM.

> Brett saw how something that was beautiful done close to the bull was ridiculous if it were done a little way off. . . . Romero had the old thing, the holding of his purity of line through the maximum of exposure, while he dominated the bull by making him realize he was unattainable, while he prepared him for the killing.
> Jake Barnes, *The Sun Also Rises*, p. 168

The next day, they get up at noon. Montoya introduces Jake to the nineteen-year-old bullfighter named Pedro Romero. In the bullfight, Romero proves to be a brave and graceful fighter and impresses everyone in the group, particularly Jake and Brett. Cohn is sickened by the goring of the horses (a ritual that begins the fights), but appreciates the rest as spectacle. On the second day of the bullfight, Romero again makes a brilliant showing of his skill as a torero. Romero does not fight on the third day and on the fourth, there is no fight.

The bullfight continues its symbolic resonance in Chapter 15. Brett notices that "something can be beautiful if done close to the bull" and ridiculous when done "a little way off" (p. 168). The same can be said of men in the novel. Those who confront their fear, as the Count had during the war and as Jake struggles to do, are braver and thus more masculine than those who try to play social games at a safe distance, like Cohn, who mopes about Brett and her relationships with other men rather than facing the reality of the situation head-on.

Chapter 16

Chapter 16 begins with bad weather, symbolic of the trouble brewing. Montoya visits Jake in his room. The innkeeper is upset. Romero has received an invitation from the American ambassador and Montoya does not know what to do. He fears that mixing with Americans will ruin Romero as a bullfighter. Jake solves the dilemma for Montoya by telling him not to deliver the message. Montoya is grateful for the advice.

Jake goes looking for his friends and ends up in the café where they are dining. Pedro Romero and a bullfighting critic are at the table next to them. Romero invites Jake to join them. Mike, who is drunk, frequently interjects obnoxious statements about bulls having no balls and Brett wanting to see how Romero gets into the green pants he wears when fighting the bulls. Montoya passes and notices Romero talking with Brett at a table covered with drinks. Angry that Jake has placed the promising young torero in such company, Montoya snubs Jake.

> "I know it," Romero said. "I'm never going to die."
> I tapped with my finger-tips on the table. Romero saw it. He shook his head.
> "No. Don't do that. The bulls are my best friends."
> I translated to Brett.
> "You kill your friends?" she asked.
> "Always," he said in English, and laughed. "So they don't kill me."
> *The Sun Also Rises*, p. 186

Cohn and Mike nearly get into a fight, but Jake intervenes, leading Mike away in a series of actions that mirror the bullfight. Brett and Bill soon join them. Later, the gang regroups for drinks (now joined by Edna, a friend of Bill's). When Mike, Bill, and Edna head off, Brett insults Cohn so that he will leave her alone with Jake. Jake admits that he still loves her and she confesses her love for Romero. They eventually locate Romero in the café, where he is sitting with other bullfighters. He makes his way over and Jake negotiates his way out of the situation, leaving Romero and Brett alone, but only after Romero and Jake exchange a knowing look that lets Romero know it is okay to pursue Brett. When Jake returns, Romero and Brett have gone.

The sexual tension builds. Mike tries to drive Cohn away by insulting him mercilessly, but Cohn refuses to leave. All three men—Jake, Mike, and Cohn—want Brett, but none can control her, which makes her attraction to the young bullfighter more poignant. Romero gracefully controls the bulls in the ring, which is one of the qualities that attracted Brett to him.

Chapter 17

Jake finds Bill, Mike, and Edna outside a bar. They had been thrown out after some Englishmen in the bar had recognized Mike. Jake suspects that Mike probably owed them money. He takes them all for a drink. Cohn shows up looking for Brett. At first, no one will tell him where she is, and then Mike reveals that she has gone off with Romero. Irate, Cohn calls Jake a pimp for introducing Brett to Romero and a fight breaks out. Jake takes a swing at Cohn, but Cohn, the better fighter, knocks Jake out and then knocks down Mike.

> I swung at him [Cohn] and he ducked. I saw his face duck sideways in the light. He hit me and I sat down on the pavement. As I started to get on my feet he hit me twice. I went down backward under a table. I tried to get up and felt I did not have any legs. I felt I must get on my feet and try to hit him. Mike helped me up. Some one poured a carafe of water on my head. Mike had an arm around me, and I found I was sitting on a chair.
>
> Jake Barnes, *The Sun Also Rises*, p. 191

Woozy from the fight, Jake returns to his hotel room. Bill shows up and asks Jake to go see Cohn. Reluctantly, Jake goes to Cohn's room. Cohn is crying. He apologizes to Jake, confessing that he has been driven crazy by his love for Brett. Jake is unsympathetic, but accepts Cohn's apology for the fight. Cohn says he is leaving in the morning.

The next day, a twenty-eight-year-old man is gored to death in the running of the bulls. Two days later a funeral service is held, and the man's wife and two children trail his coffin through the streets. The bull that gored the man is killed by Romero that afternoon. Romero makes a gift of the bull's ear to Brett as a sign of his affection. She wraps it in Jake's handkerchief and stuffs it in the drawer of a bed table in her room, oblivious to the immensity of the honor Romero has bestowed upon her.

Later, Bill and Mike show up at Jake's room and Jake learns that Cohn had found Romero and Brett together and had badly beaten Romero.

Chapter 17 marks Cohn's fall. In physically attacking the other men, he has violated a masculine code that calls for fair treatment of one's friends. As a former boxer, he is a better fighter than the others, but he lacks grace and thereby violates the unspoken rules of the game, exacerbating the already strained relationship he had with Jake and the others. Cohn's failure marks the novel's climax.

Chapter 18

Chapter 18 begins the novel's denouement, as the town prepares for the last day of the fiesta. Cohn has left and Brett is noticeably relieved. Mike is drunk and bitter over Brett's relationship with Romero. Eventually, he falls into a drunken sleep in his room. Meanwhile, Brett tries to pray in the church, but feels out of place.

> It was the first time I had seen her in the old happy, careless way since before she went off with Cohn.
> Jake Barnes, *The Sun Also Rises*, p. 209

At the bullfight, Romero makes an impressive showing with his third bull, despite the beating he took from Cohn. He gives another ear to Brett, who held his cape during both fights. Back at the hotel, Brett leaves Jake and Bill to meet Romero. Over a lunch of hard-boiled eggs and beer, Jake confesses to Bill that he feels like hell. Bill plies him with absinthe to help his depression, but it does no good. Jake gets drunker than he has ever been. When he goes upstairs to check on Brett, Mike tells him that she left with Romero. Jake naps and then joins Bill and Mike in the dining room. The chapter ends with a sense of despair as Jake remarks, "The three of us sat at the table, and it seemed as though about six people were missing" (p. 224).

Book III

Chapter 19

The day after the fiesta, Jake, Bill, and Mike rent a car and travel to Bayonne. Mike, who is down to his last twenty francs (after doling out heavy tips to a bartender), is headed for Saint Jean de Luz where he can live on credit until his next check comes in. Bill is returning to Paris. The next day, Jake catches the train for San Sebastian, where he plans to spend the next week. His plans are disrupted when he receives two desperate telegrams from Brett—one forwarded from Pamplona and one forwarded from Paris—asking him to meet her at the Hotel Montana in Madrid. He dutifully obliges.

> "You know it makes one feel rather good deciding not to be a b---h." [Brett said.]
> "Yes." [Jake said.]
> "It's sort of what we have instead of God."
> "Some people have God," I [Jake] said. "Quite a lot."
> "He never worked very well with me."
> *The Sun Also Rises*, p. 245

In Madrid, he learns that Brett has left Romero and plans to return to Mike. Although she says she does not want to talk about the affair, the conversation keeps circling back to her reasons for leaving him: his age (he is nineteen and Brett is thirty-four), his lack of experience (he had only been with two women before), the bad influence she might have on his bullfighting, and his desire to change her (he wants her to grow her hair long and marry him).

Jake and Brett go to dinner. Afterward, they take a cab ride through Madrid. She leans comfortably against him. She says, "Oh, Jake, . . . we could have had such a damned good time together." To which he responds, "Yes. . . . Isn't it pretty to think so?" (p. 247).

Techniques, Themes, and Metaphors in *The Sun Also Rises*

Iceberg Theory

Hemingway's writing technique is frequently compared to an iceberg—an object that moves gracefully, with a sense of mass, but of which only one-eighth is visible. Hemingway explains this technique in *Death in the Afternoon*, in which he writes,

> If a writer of prose knows enough about what he is writing about he may omit things that he knows and the reader, if the writer is writing truly enough, will have a feeling of those things as strongly as though the writer had stated them. The dignity of movement of an iceberg is due to only one-eighth of it being above water. (p. 192)

The iceberg theory relates to how much information Hemingway manages to get across without literally writing it. Perhaps the most salient example is found in the character of Jake Barnes. He acknowledges but does not complain about his wound, yet we sense that the scope of his dilemma is broad and the psychological pain he experiences because he cannot consummate his love with Brett runs deep.

In Hemingway's fiction, readers sense the seven-eighths that are unspoken from the one-eighth that is shown, thus increasing the weight of what is said. This is readily apparent when in the last line of the novel Jake responds to Brett's claim that they "could have had such a damned good time together" by saying, "Isn't it pretty to think so?" This line recapitulates the emotional content of the entire novel. It applies to Robert Cohn's behavior toward Brett, whom he thinks could love him, and Jake, whom he believes is a good friend. It applies to Brett as she casually amuses herself with each of her lovers. It applies to Jake, who at points poses the possibility of himself and Brett getting together despite his wound. The last line leaves us with an understanding of the disparity that remains between what is experienced and how one thinks about what is experienced.

> I thought I had paid for everything. Not like the woman pays and pays and pays. No idea of retribution or punishment. Just exchange of values. You gave up something and got something else. Or you worked for something. You paid some way for everything that was any good. I paid my way into enough things that I liked, so that I had a good time. Either you paid by learning about them, or by experience, or by taking chances, or by money. Enjoying living was learning to get your money's worth and knowing when you had it. . . . It seemed like a fine philosophy. In five years, I thought, it will seem just as silly as all the other fine philosophies I've had.
>
> Jake Barnes, *The Sun Also Rises*, p. 148

The Code of Living

Hemingway claimed *The Sun Also Rises* to be a "moral book." He told Archibald MacLeish in 1943 that he had successfully embodied in the novel the theme that promiscuity was no solution. The novel is about a generation of men and women who returned from the war emotionally, physically, and spiritually wounded, men and women who were disillusioned by the political unrest that followed and who had lost faith with tradition, a generation that Gertrude Stein is credited with labeling "The Lost Generation." This generation, detached from its history, drank too much, partied, engaged in sexual escapades, and appeared, to conventional eyes, to be purposeless.

All the main characters in *The Sun Also Rises* struggle to lessen their individual pains by engaging in behaviors that the mainstream of American culture (such as Hemingway's parents) found objectionable. But the thrust of *The Sun Also Rises* is not the chronicling of immoral behavior. The novel's Lost Generation characters are searching for a new morality, a new way of existing in the world to replace the failed systems that preceded them. Hemingway realized that "all generations were lost by something and always had been and always would be" (*A Moveable Feast*, p. 30).

The characters in *The Sun Also Rises* cannot find morality in church or politics. They are searching for new standards, a new code for behavior. Scholar Scott Donaldson points out that it is "Jake Barnes who explicitly states the code of Hemingway's 'very moral' novel." Donaldson argues that the code by which the characters live (or *should* live) is based on a fair and equitable exchange.

When Jake returns to France at the end of the novel, he notes that in France "everything is on such a clear financial basis" (p. 233). He gives the waiters large tips and they give him friendship—"No one makes things complicated by becoming your friend for any obscure reason" (p. 233). This simple principle, or code, explains all the failed relationships in the novel: Jake and Brett cannot be together because there is no fair exchange. Jake admits that he has gotten something for nothing from Brett. His wound has made it impossible for him to return to her an amount of affection equal to what he gets from her. Jake and Cohn's friendship suffers because Cohn gives less to Jake than he expects from Jake. Even Brett, when she leaves

Romero, realizes that to continue in a relationship with him would not be a fair exchange of value—she would get more from him than she could possibly return.

The relationships that survive can also be measured by this standard. Jake and Bill remain good friends because neither asks more from the other than he is willing to give. The same is true for Jake and Georgette. Even Brett's decision to return to the drunken, bankrupt Mike, though pitiful, can be seen as a fair exchange of values considering Brett's inability to remain loyal to him.

Hemingway's code in *The Sun Also Rises* is perhaps best seen in Romero's relationships with the bulls. Romero claims that the bulls are his "best friends" and that he kills his friends "so they don't kill" him (p. 186). The torero facing the bull in the ring is an equitable encounter. The bull wants to kill the torero (and has that chance) and the torero wants to kill the bull. In the violent algebra of the ring, their relationship is based on a fair exchange.

Jake's Wound as Symbol

E. M. Halliday points out that "Jake Barnes's war-wound impotence . . . [is a] metaphor for the whole atmosphere of sterility and frustration which is the ambiance of *The Sun Also Rises.*" Many of the characters in the novel are wounded. Brett has lost her true love in the war. Cohn is tortured by his inability to preserve his relationship with Brett. Mike is a bankrupt failure. The wound (and resulting impotence) that Jake carries with him symbolizes the psychic and physical wounds of all the young people who survived the war, wounds that have left them powerless to embrace the ideals they once valued.

Chapter 2

The Old Man and the Sea

Background on the Writing of *The Old Man and the Sea*

Hemingway completed the manuscript of *The Old Man and the Sea* (then called the Santiago story) in 1951. First planned as part of three long short stories, then as the fourth part of a four-part book on the sea that he worked on for some time, the manuscript eventually developed a life of its own. The moment he began showing copies to friends in 1951 and 1952, it was clear that Hemingway had produced something special. The story had a "'mysterious quality' not present in his other work."

The story had been brewing in Hemingway's mind for many years. Its predecessor was a short story called "On the Blue Water", which had been published in *Esquire* in 1936. By 1939 he had a clear vision of the work as a detailed story outlining the adventure of an elderly fisherman who snags a marlin after four days of effort, but cannot get the large fish into his boat. During the trip back to land, sharks steal his prize.

Hemingway got the idea for the story while living in Cuba, where he frequently fished and drank with Cuban fishermen. According to Hemingway's brother, Leicester, Hemingway insisted that "he had created *The Old Man and the Sea* out of years on the water, and from his knowledge of dozens of fishermen."

Many consider *The Old Man and the Sea* to be Hemingway's masterpiece.

The Old Man and the Sea came at an opportune time for Hemingway. Michael Reynolds describes Hemingway in 1951 as "fifty-one years old, sicker than most knew, and eleven years without a successful novel." Hemingway's previous novel, *Across the River and Into the Trees* (1950) had not been received favorably and many were beginning to believe that Hemingway's better days as a writer were behind him. *The Old Man and the Sea* proved them wrong, much to Hemingway's satisfaction, and was heralded as a masterpiece by almost everyone who read it.

Santiago, the old man of *The Old Man and the Sea*, had much in common with Hemingway. Like Hemingway, he had gone a long time without success (eighty-four days without a fish), and struggled against time and nature to show he had not been defeated. Hemingway, for whom writing had become increasingly difficult, struggled to demonstrate that he was still a writer worthy of his reputation. *The Old Man and the Sea* made his point. Its first publication in *Life* magazine in 1952 sold over five million copies and sold out in less than forty-eight hours. It was picked up as a Book-of-the-Month Club selection and spent twenty-six weeks on the *New York Times* bestseller list. In 1953, it was awarded the Pulitzer Prize for fiction and contributed greatly to Hemingway's winning of the Nobel Prize for Literature in 1954.

Overview of The Old Man and the Sea

Opening (pages 9–25)

The Old Man and the Sea opens with the line: "He was an old man who fished alone in a skiff in the Gulf Stream and he had gone eighty-four days now without taking a fish" (p. 9). The sentence, like the novel, is simple and straightforward, yet richly establishes the main character, the setting, and the conflict. It is a wonderful example of Hemingway's ability to distill language down to its purest form without sacrificing content.

During the first day, we meet Santiago, an elderly fisherman who has been unlucky. Santiago is poor. He lives in a bare shack. His shirt has been patched many times, as have the sails of his boat. His companion and only friend is a boy named Manolin. The boy had fished with Santiago since the age of five and had learned fishing from the old man, but after forty days with no fish, the boy's father made him join the crew of another boat.

In the opening of the story, the boy nurtures the old man, bringing him beer, food, and bait for the next day's fishing. The boy does not feel pity for the old fisherman; he feels respect and a sense of responsibility as evident in the following passage about the old man washing before eating the meal the boy has brought him:

> Where did you wash? the boy thought. The village water supply was two streets down the road. I must have water here for him, the boy thought, and soap and a good towel. Why am I so thoughtless? I must get him another shirt and a jacket for the winter and some sort of shoes and another blanket. (p. 21)

Santiago and the boy discuss baseball as they eat, and the boy expresses his confidence in Santiago's skill as a fisherman. Afterward, Santiago agrees to wake the boy in the morning, the boy leaves, and Santiago falls to sleep. He dreams of Africa and the "harbors and roadsteads of the Canary Islands" (p. 25).

Day 1 (pages 25–53)

Before sunrise Santiago walks to the boy's house, wakes him, and the boy helps the old man carry his line, harpoon, and gaff to the old man's boat. The two have coffee. The boy wishes the old man good luck, and the old man rows through the dark waters and out of the harbor with only a bottle of water to last him the day.

The old man's plan for the day is to fish far out. On the moonlit ocean, he thinks about how the young people think of the sea as masculine, as "a contestant or a place or even an enemy," but that he thinks of her as feminine, "something that gave or withheld great favours" (p. 30). After the sun rises, he sees a man-of-war bird circling a school of dolphins. The old man follows the bird. The dolphins move away from him too fast for him to have any hope of hooking one, but the bird leads the old man to a school of tuna, from which he snags a ten-pound fish. He plans to use it as bait.

> "Fish," he said softly, aloud, "I'll stay with you until I am dead."
> He'll stay with me too, I suppose, the old man thought and he waited for it to be light.
> *The Old Man and the Sea,* p. 52

The old man hooks a large marlin around noon. The marlin pulls the boat and the old man farther out to sea. After four hours, the fish shows no signs of weakening. It continues to pull him out to sea into the night. Santiago wishes he had the boy with him. "No one should be alone in their old age," he thinks (p. 48).

The old man admires and pities the fish and wonders if the fish is "as desperate" as the old man (p. 49). When another fish takes one of the other lines the old man is trailing, the old man cuts the line and attaches the remaining line to the line for the marlin. Working alone in the dark, he cuts his other lines, adding all remaining lines to the marlin's line. He vows to stay with the great fish to the end.

Day 2 (pages 53–86)

The old man's second day battling the fish begins. The fish shows no signs of tiring and has yet to break the surface of the water. Everything the old man knows of the fish he reasons from the feel of the line that is strapped across his back, the line feeding through his hands. At one point, a bird rests for a short time on the line, but flies away when the fish jerks the line, cutting the old man's hand. The old man realizes the marlin has begun to slow.

To keep his strength and relieve the cramping in his hand, the old man eats some of the tuna he caught earlier, but the hand that had been holding the line is rigid and he cannot uncurl the fingers. Finally the marlin breaks water and Santiago learns that the fish is larger than any he has seen or heard about—two feet longer than his boat and more than one thousand pounds.

The old man's hand uncramps and he prays that he will catch the fish. The day wears on and he recalls a hand-wrestling match he had won as a younger man. The match had lasted from Sunday morning until Monday morning, and the old man had persevered.

Just before dark, the old man catches a dolphin on the other line he had dropped into the water when he realized he would need more to eat. He pulls the dolphin into the boat. Then he considers lashing the oars across the boat's stern to increase the drag on the marlin, which is still moving steadily through the water as the sun sets on another day. Still keeping the weight of the line across his back, the old man guts the dolphin, eating part of a filet and one of two flying fish that he finds whole in the dolphin's belly.

The old man rigs the line and gets some sleep, his hand still on the line so he will know when it moves. He dreams of porpoises, his bed in the village, and lions on the beaches of Africa. A jerk in the line awakens him, the line speeding through his hands as the marlin breaks water and makes a run. Breaking water a dozen times, the marlin tires and moves into the current. The old man knows that his moment is coming. He eats the remaining flying fish for strength as the sun begins to rise.

Day 3 (pages 86–122)
Shortly after the sun rises on the old man's third day of battling the fish, the marlin begins to circle, a sign that he has weakened and the fight is nearly over. The old man pushes himself beyond his limits, pulling in line each time the fish circles. He works without rest until around noon when the fish is near enough to the boat for him to drive his harpoon into the fish's heart.

The marlin is much larger than the man had first suspected—about 1,500 pounds—too large to get into the boat. He straps the fish to the side of the boat and raises his patched sails and sets his course southwest, confident that he will be able to navigate back to land. He has no food and is nearly out of water so he hooks a patch of gulf weed and eats the shrimp he shakes from it.

> "But man is not made for defeat," he [Santiago] said. "A man can be destroyed but not defeated." I am sorry that I killed the fish though, he thought. Now the bad time is coming and I do not even have the harpoon.
> *The Old Man and the Sea*, p. 103

An hour into the trip home a large Mako shark appears. It takes a bite out of the marlin before Santiago drives his harpoon into the shark's brain, killing it, but losing the harpoon in the process. He rigs a new weapon from his knife and one of the oars. Two hours later, two shovel-nosed sharks appear, drawn by the scent of the fish. The old man kills one with his makeshift harpoon, but only after the shark has taken some of the marlin. The second shark feeds on the fish from below and the old man has to maneuver to get the shark to surface, where the old man punches and stabs him. After both sharks are dead, the old man notices that one-quarter of the marlin has been eaten.

Next, another shovel-nosed shark hits the marlin. The old man gets his knife into the shark's brain, but the blade snaps in the process. Around sunset, he beats off two more sharks, but at the price of more of his prized catch. Half the fish is now gone.

The sun sets, and the old man looks for the glow of Havana. It appears around ten o'clock. At midnight or so, the sharks come again. This time they are in a pack, it is dark, and he has no weapon. He beats at them blindly until one tears the club from his hands, and then he begins to beat them with the tiller. The tiller breaks against the head of the last shark and the battle is over—the meat of the fish is gone.

Beaten, he makes port. Taking his mast and sail with him, he heads for home, the remains of the fish still lashed to his boat. He drags himself home and falls asleep.

Day 4 (pages 122–127)

In the morning, the boy finds the old man asleep in his bed and weeps over the old man's wounds. The boat has been discovered with the eighteen-foot marlin attached. The people of the town are impressed by the size of the old man's catch and saddened by his loss.

The boy gets coffee for the old man. When the man awakens, the boy says he will return to fishing with the old man and that he will prepare the boat for fishing while the old man recovers. The old man tells the boy that he can have the sword of the marlin.

Later, a pair of tourists sees the spine and tail of the marlin lying with garbage. They ask the waiter what it is, but misunderstand when he responds and mistakenly assume it is a shark tail.

Up the road, the old man is sleeping and dreaming of lions as the boy watches over him.

Significant Elements and Readings of *The Old Man and the Sea*

One of the strengths of *The Old Man and the Sea* is its openness to interpretation. Many critical approaches are rewarded and many views can be supported by the text. Some have read the book as Christian allegory, pointing to numerous allusions in the text that parallel the life of Christ. The name Santiago is Spanish for St. James, one of the original disciples of Jesus. The bleeding wounds on Santiago's hands recall stigmata—the wounds of Christ. Santiago stumbles as he carries his wooden mast through the streets, and Christ stumbled carrying the cross. Furthermore, the novel carries numerous religious references. Santiago is a man who does not have an "understanding" of sin and Jesus was reportedly a man who did not know sin (cf. p. 105). One critic, Ignatius M. Melito, argues that Santiago is portrayed as a "Christ-figure" and that this portrayal gives the character "some or all of his significance from the historically established meaning of the figure of Christ."

However, reading the novel as a straight allegory may be an oversimplification. E. M. Halliday points out that characters such as Santiago "disclaim their religiosity, and their Hail Marys are uttered mechanically enough to evoke a chilly memory of the sleepless waiter in [Hemingway's story] 'A Clean Well-Lighted Place,' who prayed, 'Hail nothing, full of nothing, nothing is with thee.'"

We might also read *The Old Man and the Sea* as a statement of common Hemingway themes, as Patricia Dunlavy Valenti suggests: "A man may be destroyed but not defeated. . . . Santiago demonstrates the 'grace under pressure' of the Hemingway 'code hero,' a man who tenaciously adheres to the rules of whatever game he may be playing, notwithstanding his apparent defeat." As Arthur Waldhorn points out,

> Doom is not, in Hemingway's vision, to be identified with defeat. All creatures share doom. Knowing this breeds humility in man, the reverence Santiago feels for the marlin alive and dead. Defeat means yielding to doom without a struggle, abandoning, in effect, the pride that makes it worthwhile to be a man.

Much can be made of the symbolism in *The Old Man and the Sea*, and it is tempting to make a great deal of Hemingway's straightforward prose, but whatever Hemingway's intention or design, it is fair to say of the work, as Waldhorn does, that "Rarely has exposition been more lucid, description more evocative, or both so relevant to emotive and thematic force."

Chapter 3

The Other Novels

The Torrents of Spring

The Torrents of Spring was published in May 1926. It is technically Hemingway's first novel, though it was greatly overshadowed by the publication of *The Sun Also Rises* later in the year. The book parodies the writing of Hemingway's contemporaries, primarily Sherwood Anderson's *Dark Laughter* and Gertrude Stein's *The Making of Americans*. Both Anderson and Stein were friends of Hemingway, contributed greatly to his writing style, and helped open doors for the young writer. Nevertheless, Hemingway, despite opposition from virtually everyone, went ahead with the publication of the book.

The Torrents of Spring tells of two men and their search for their destiny. Scripps O'Neil is a naïve and bewildered writer who marries one waitress, only to leave her for Mandy, a more literate waitress. Scripps meets Yogi Johnson when Scripps takes a job at a pump factory in Petoskey, Michigan. Yogi is a World War I veteran who has lost interest in women. When Yogi encounters an Indian squaw wearing only a pair of moccasins, his interest in women returns and he leaves with her.

A Farewell to Arms

Hemingway knew he needed a strong book after the success of *The Sun Also Rises*. When he delivered the manuscript of *A Farewell to Arms* to Max Perkins, Perkins considered it magnificent and offered him "the largest sum *Scribners Magazine* had ever yet paid" for the serialization rights.

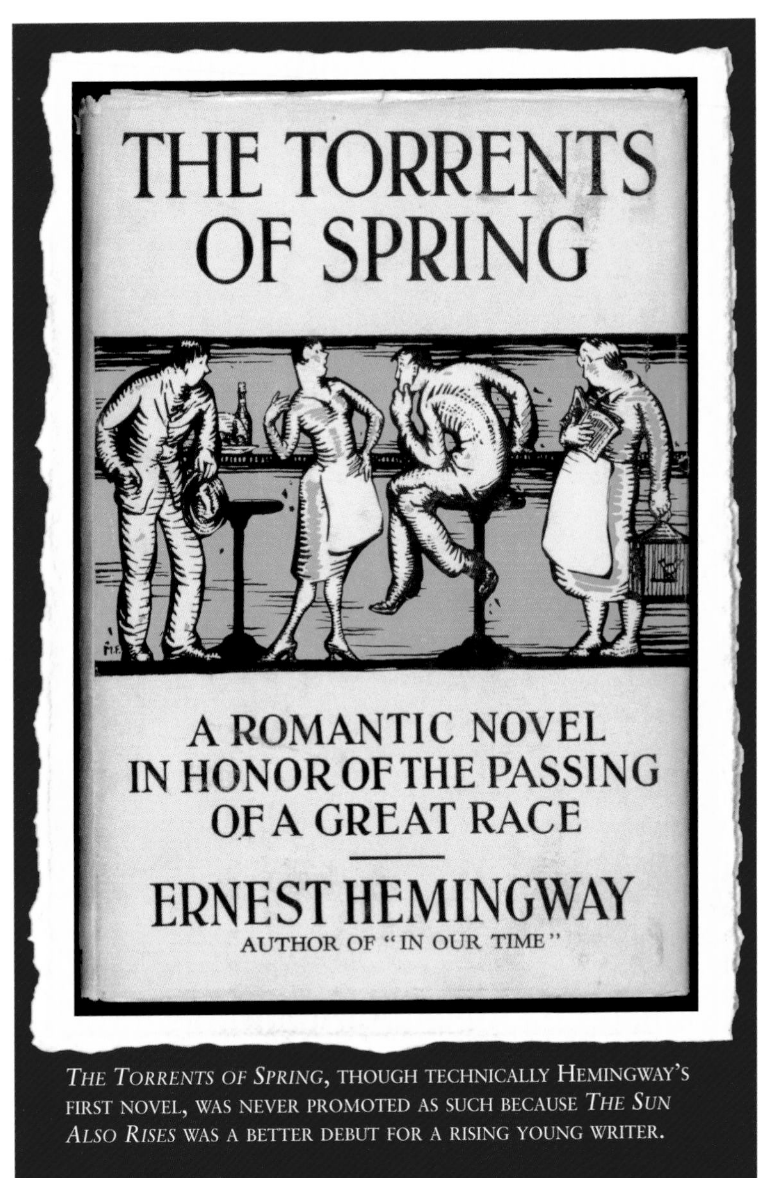

The Torrents of Spring, though technically Hemingway's first novel, was never promoted as such because *The Sun Also Rises* was a better debut for a rising young writer.

Although it is not directly biographical, the story was inspired by Agnes von Kurowsky, the nurse Hemingway met and fell in love with while hospitalized for wounds he suffered working for the ambulance corps during World War I. Kurowsky inspired the character of Catherine Barkley in the novel, while Lieutenant Frederic Henry is modeled on Hemingway. Like Hemingway, Henry is an American ambulance driver during World War I.

The novel is divided into five books. Book One covers Henry's experiences up to and including his wounding by a mortar shell. In Book Two, Henry is in an Italian hospital, where he meets Catherine. They fall in love and Catherine becomes pregnant. Their time together is interrupted when the head nurse finds brandy bottles in his room. She accuses him of intentionally delaying his recovery, his leave is cancelled, and he is returned to the front. In Book Three, Henry returns to the chaos of war and becomes disillusioned with the conflict, declaring that he "had seen nothing sacred, and the things that were glorious had no glory and the sacrifices were like the stockyards at Chicago if nothing was done with the meat except to bury it" (p. 185). While in retreat, he narrowly escapes being executed for desertion, and makes his way back to Milan. In Book Four, Henry reunites with Catherine. Aware that the Italian police plan to arrest Henry in the morning, he and Catherine escape in a rowboat to Switzerland. There they rent a house. In Book Five, Henry and Catherine are together in Switzerland awaiting the birth of their child. In the end, Catherine checks into a hospital. She goes into labor, but the baby will not come. The doctor performs a caesarean. The novel ends tragically because the baby is stillborn, Catherine dies from complications, and Henry walks "back to the hotel in the rain" (p. 332). Hemingway's ending, Bernard Oldsey notes, is "one of the most famous segments in American fiction."

A Farewell to Arms was considered a magnificent successor to *The Sun Also Rises*. It was later made into a blockbuster movie starring Rock Hudson.

The end of *A Farewell to Arms* highlights one of Hemingway's most important thematic elements. Hemingway reminds us that the ultimate destination for everyone is death. Through Catherine, Henry realizes that "they get you in the end." You never get "away with anything." Suffering and loss are "what people got for loving each other" (p. 320). Catherine dreamed that she would die in the rain, and she has, leaving Henry to embrace the lesson he has learned. Waldhorn points out that "when Henry admits that kissing Catherine's dead lips 'was like saying goodbye to a statue,' he is done with illusion. That stage of his apprenticeship ends as he walks into the rain." Life is not fair, yet Frederic Henry endures even in the face of great loss.

To Have and Have Not

To Have and Have Not was published in 1937, eight years after *A Farewell to Arms*. Hemingway's public was thrilled to have a new novel to read, but the critical reception was not favorable. Malcolm Cowley considered it one of Hemingway's "weakest" books. Writer Delmore Schwartz called it "a stupid and foolish book, a disgrace to a good writer, a book which should never have been printed."

The novel is divided into three sections: "Harry Morgan (Spring)," "Harry Morgan (Fall)," and "Harry Morgan (Winter)." The protagonist, Harry Morgan, owns a fishing boat that he has used to run contraband and charters out to fishermen. He is married, has three daughters, and lives in Key West. In the first section, Harry is trying to avoid illegal ventures. He charters his boat to a wealthy, narcissistic man who loses an expensive reel belonging to Harry and then skips out without paying for the charter. The financial setback forces Harry to take an illegal run. He agrees to transport twelve aliens from Havana to Florida, but ends up killing the man who hired him and dropping the aliens on the nearest beach before returning home to his wife.

In the second section, Harry and a mate (Wesley) are shot at by Cuban authorities while transporting a run of illegal liquor from Cuba to Key West. They manage to get the boat back to the Keys, but only after dumping their cargo and receiving help from a friend who is captain of another fishing charter.

In the third section, Harry has lost his arm to the wound he received from the Cuban authorities, who also confiscated his boat. Desperate for money, Harry agrees to transport four Cubans from Key West to Cuba. Harry's four passengers are bank robbers who rob the local bank and plan to use the money to finance the Cuban revolution. On the way, Harry manages to kill all four, but not before being wounded again. The novel ends with Harry relating his views on life to the Coast Guard and his wife's sorrowful reaction to Harry's death in the hospital.

To Have and Have Not is notable as the only one of Hemingway's novels to take place in the United States, and the only one to confront social issues. The title itself refers to class divisions between the wealthy and the poor—the *haves* and the *have nots*.

For Whom the Bell Tolls

For Whom the Bell Tolls, published in 1940, was a tremendous financial and critical success, Hemingway's first major success since *A Farewell to Arms*. It received some negative reviews, but the reaction among critics was generally positive. The work has come to be viewed by most as one of Hemingway's masterpieces. J. Donald Adams in his *New York Times* review called the novel "the best book Ernest Hemingway has written, the fullest, the deepest, the truest" and predicted that it would become "one of the major novels in American literature."

The novel is set during three days of the Spanish Civil War. The protagonist, Robert Jordan, is an American volunteer who has come to Spain to help the Loyalist effort against the fascists. Jordan is assigned to dynamite a bridge as part of a planned attack. He joins up with a band of partisan fighters led by Pablo, a coward and troublemaker who frequently locks horns with Jordan. Pablo's wife, Pilar, turns out to be stronger than her husband.

Also with the band is María, a young woman who was rescued from the fascists when the partisans blew up the train she was on. María and Jordan fall in love as plans are laid for Jordan to complete his mission. At one point, Pablo runs off with some of the dynamite, but he returns, claiming that he is no coward and that he will help destroy the bridge. On the final day, the fighters attack the bridge and Jordan attaches the dynamite. The bridge explodes successfully, but during their retreat, Jordan's horse is shot from underneath him. His leg is shattered during the fall. Unable to travel, he convinces María to go with the others. Alone in the end, Jordan waits with a machine gun for the fascists, intending to buy María and the fighters some time before he is killed.

Scholar Peter Messent argues that Robert Jordan is one of Hemingway's most fully realized characters, stating that, "In Robert Jordan's figure and his thoughts, positive and heroic individualism are fully realized. . . . Any sense of uncertainty on the subject's part is worked through and overcome in the course of the novel." This differentiates Jordan from Hemingway's previous heroes and represents an artistic advance in Hemingway's fiction.

Across the River and Into the Trees

Across the River and Into the Trees was serialized in *Cosmopolitan* magazine and then published by Scribners in September 1950. Many consider it the weakest of the novels published during Hemingway's lifetime. J. Donald Adams said in his *New York Times* article that the reviews were decidedly negative, noting that out of eleven reviews only "three were definitely favorable."

Adams wrote:

> To me, *Across the River and Into the Trees* is one of the saddest books I have ever read; not because I am moved to compassion by the conjunction of love and death in the Colonel's life, but because a great talent has come, whether for now or forever, to such a dead end.

Some reviewers did like the novel. Famous novelist John O'Hara staunchly defended Hemingway and the novel against the critics, calling Hemingway the most important author "since the death of Shakespeare."

The story takes place on a single Sunday. Fifty-year-old Colonel Richard Cantwell is duck-hunting. Cantwell, who has already had four heart attacks, realizes that the end of his life is approaching. From his duck blind, he recollects his life, particularly his military career and his love for Renata, an eighteen-year-old Italian contessa. The novel is a journey into a seasoned soldier's mind as he attempts to face death with dignity. At the end, he dies of a heart attack on his way back to Trieste, Italy, one Sunday evening.

The Posthumous Novels: *Islands in the Stream, The Garden of Eden,* and *True at First Light*

When Hemingway died in 1961, he left behind four unfinished, book-length manuscripts. One was his memoir of his life in Paris in the 1920s, which was published as *A Moveable Feast* in 1964. The other three were unfinished novels, which have since been published as *Islands in the Stream* (1970), *The Garden of Eden* (1986), and *True at First Light* (1999).

The Garden of Eden and *Islands in the Stream* were part of a larger work that Hemingway had been writing since 1945, which he referred to as "The Land, Sea,

ERNEST HEMINGWAY WROTE ABOUT WHAT HE KNEW. WHEN NOT WRITING, HE LOVED TO FISH AND VISIT EXOTIC LOCALES SUCH AS AFRICA.

and Air Book." This work included writing that became *Across the River and Into the Trees* and *The Old Man and the Sea*. Rose Marie Burwell argues that the writing that became the three novels and the memoir

> form a tetralogy that is Hemingway's portrait of the artist as writer and painter, and as son, husband, and father; but their serial nature, and their place in the body of his fiction, has been unrecognized, misconstrued and undervalued because of the manuscript deletions made for publication, the order in which the three published works appeared, and the restrictions of archival material that clarifies much about their composition and intentions.

Islands in the Stream (as published) was divided into three sections: "Bimini," "Cuba," and "At Sea." The three sections are scantly related, rendering the novel fragmented, though this fragmentation has more to do with editing than with Hemingway. Thomas Hudson is the main character in all three sections. Hudson is a successful landscape painter of scenes in Bimini in the Bahamas. "Bimini" deals with Hudson's relationship with his three sons, two of whom die at the close of the section. In "Cuba," Hudson is in Havana, where he uses his fishing boat to hunt German submarines and grieves over the loss of his third son, Tom. "At Sea" details Hudson's search for the crew of a downed German submarine. In the end, Hudson is seriously wounded and expects to die.

The Garden of Eden also suffered from editing. The manuscript that Hemingway left behind was around 200,000 words. It was edited down to 70,000 words for publication, which some critics claim damaged the integrity of the work. Nevertheless, *The Garden of Eden* remains Hemingway's most unusual work. It involves writer David Bourne's complicated marriage to Catherine, a bisexual woman who, shortly after their wedding, cuts her hair and begins dressing like a man, asking David to assume a more feminine role. As a result, they both experiment with gender role reversal.

In the south of France, Catherine becomes involved with a lesbian named Marita. Catherine invites Marita into her relationship with David. Eventually, David and Marita grow close and Catherine becomes jealous, but Catherine is mostly bothered by the African story that David is writing, which she believes is drawing his attention away from her. In the end, she burns the story and leaves David and Marita together. In her absence, David sets out to rewrite the African story from memory.

The posthumous publication of *The Garden of Eden* in 1986 led to a revitalization of Hemingway scholarship among feminist scholars. Often criticized in the 1970s and early 1980s for what was seen as misogynist tendencies in his writing, Hemingway's work was revisited in light of what *The Garden of Eden* revealed about his understanding of women. This reevaluation of Hemingway's treatment of women characters led scholar Linda Patterson Miller to justify Hemingway's "sketchy" women characters by claiming that "he discovered them more fully by giving them little to say," and that they "embody the 7/8 of the iceberg that is down under."

True at First Light is more difficult to classify than *Islands in the Stream* and *The Garden of Eden.* Hemingway had long referred to the unfinished manuscript as "The Africa Book." He began it in 1954 while on his second African safari. Carlos Baker, his biographer, describes the origin of the work as follows:

> As fall approached he began a series of stories based on his recent experiences in Africa. One of them expanded so steadily under his hand that he thought it might become a novel. In fact it was more like a slightly fictionized [*sic*] day-to-day diary of the safari, almost completely formless, filled with scenes that ranged from the fairly effective to the banal.

Hemingway's son, Patrick, edited the unfinished manuscript into *True at First Light*, which was published in 1999 in celebration of the centennial of Hemingway's birth. A scholarly edition, edited by Robert W. Lewis and Robert E. Fleming, appeared as *Under Kilimanjaro* in 2005. The book recounts—and reshapes—Hemingway's experiences in Africa with his fourth wife, Mary. A great deal of the attention the book received when it was published focused on speculation about the recounting of the author taking an African bride. Nobel Prize–

winning author Nadine Gordimer condemned the publication of posthumous books and this prying interest in Hemingway's life. She called it "an insult . . . to his lifelong integrity to his art to regard his work in this shabby prurient way," and said, "On Ernest Hemingway's centennial . . . too much will be speculated about him, too much spoken about him, too much written about him, including my own part in this. When we go home, let us leave his life alone. It belongs to him, as he lived it. Let us read his books."

Chapter 4

Other Writings

Hemingway achieved notoriety and his greatest fame as a writer of novels, beginning with the publication of *The Sun Also Rises* when he was twenty-six years old. But Hemingway was always a marvelous writer of short fiction. In the early days of his career, he thought of himself as a short story writer and did not plan to become a novelist as well. By the time his first two novels were published in 1926, he had already published a collection of short stories (*In Our Time*, 1924) and another of short stories and poetry (*Three Stories and Ten Poems*, 1923). He followed the publication of his first two novels with another short story collection (*Men Without Women*, 1927). Each of his next two novels was also followed by a short story collection.

Gabriel García Márquez, the Nobel Prize–winning author of *One Hundred Years of Solitude*, credits Heming-way as one of the two writers who most influenced him as a young man (the other was William Faulkner). García Márquez considers Hemingway primarily a short story writer, preferring his short stories to his novels. García Márquez says of Hemingway's work:

> All of Hemingway's work shows that his spirit was brilliant but short-lived. And it is understandable. An internal tension like his, subjected to such a severe dominance of technique, can't be sustained within the vast and hazardous reaches of a novel. It was his nature, and his error was to

> try to exceed his own splendid limits. And that is why everything superfluous is more noticeable in him than in other writers. His novels are like short stories that are out of proportion, that include too much. In contrast, the best thing about his stories is that they give the impression something is missing, and this is precisely what confers their mystery and their beauty.

García Márquez is not alone in his assessment. Many others feel that Hemingway's star shone brightest in his short stories. Scholar Paul Smith argues that Hemingway's short fiction "was his real genius."

Hemingway's first mature short story was "Up in Michigan," which he wrote in Paris in 1921. He produced a regular stream of short stories up to the time when his health began to fade, including some of the most well-known works in modern American literature.

"Hills Like White Elephants" (1927)

Hemingway wrote "Hills Like White Elephants" in 1927, but writer Robert McAlmon says the idea for the story began in 1923 in Rapolla, Italy, when, during a conversation about how unfair antiabortion laws were, McAlmon "told a story of a girl who had managed to have herself taken care of." McAlmon says, "Later Hemingway informed me that my remark suggested the story." The story was first published in August 1927 in *Transition* magazine and then included in the October publication of *Men Without Women*.

The story is one of Hemingway's shortest and most widely known. It takes place in a rail junction near the Ebro River in Spain. A man identified only as the American and a woman called "Jig" are drinking beer and waiting for the train to Madrid. The two are lovers, although it is obvious their relationship is strained. They are headed to Madrid so that the woman can get an abortion.

The story is comprised almost wholly of dialogue. The most remarkable characteristic of the dialogue is what is not said. Beneath the superficially innocent conversation, the true weight of the story is carried. An excellent example of Hemingway's iceberg theory, the most important aspects are implied by what is written rather than explicitly stated, as in this excerpt:

> "You've got to realize," he said, "that I don't want you to do it if you don't want to. I'm perfectly willing to go through with it if it means anything to you."
> "Doesn't it mean anything to you? We could get along."
> "Yes, you know it's perfectly simple."
> "It's all right for you to say that, but I do know it."
> "Would you do something for me now?"
> "I'd do anything for you."
> "Would you please please please please please please please stop talking?" (*Stories*, p. 277)

The tension between the two is evident even in this brief excerpt. The American says he does not want her to have the abortion, but he does. He says he would do anything for the woman, but he won't. The American and Jig both realize that their relationship will never be the same, that it is doomed, yet they talk as if they are salvaging their love, which produces resonant ironies, such as the last line of the story, in which Jig declares, "I feel fine. . . . There's nothing wrong with me. I feel fine" (p. 278).

"Hills Like White Elephants" is considered one of Hemingway's masterpieces. It has been widely anthologized, which, Michael Reynolds notes, helped to widen "Hemingway's dedicated audience."

"The Killers" (1927)

Originally titled "The Matadors," "The Killers" is, like "Hills Like White Elephants," one of Hemingway's most anthologized and widely read stories. "The Killers" is another story notable for what it doesn't say. In "The Art of the Short Story," Hemingway said of "The Killers" that it "probably had more left out of it than anything I ever wrote."

The story takes place in two settings. The first is Henry's Eating-House, a Chicago bar that has been converted into a diner. Two hit men, Al and Max, enter the diner around 5:00 PM. After quibbling about the unavailability of items listed on the menu and settling for eggs, they force the only other patron, Nick Adams, and the cook into the back where they tie them up. George, who runs the diner, remains out front. Al waits in the back with a sawed-off shotgun at the ready, while Max remains at the front counter. They are waiting for a former boxer named Ole, who has presumably double-crossed the Chicago mob and whom they intend to kill "for a friend" (*Stories*, p. 283). Ole does not show up. When the clock reads 7:10, the two leave, and George unties the cook and Nick Adams. Nick then walks to the boardinghouse where Ole lives—the second setting in the story. Ole is in his room. He is lying on the bed and has not been out all day. Nick warns him about the two hit men, but Ole is already aware that he is being hunted and has apparently reconciled himself to his fate. Nick returns to the diner and tells George that he is going to leave town because thinking about Ole "waiting in the room and knowing he's going to get it . . . [is] too damned awful." George advises him that he had "better not think about it" (p. 289).

Some credit Hemingway with developing the type of casual, joking gangster patter that predominated crime fiction through most of the twentieth century. In 1927, when the story was first published in *Scribners Magazine*, gangsters were much in the public consciousness.

> "He comes here to eat every night, don't he?"
> "Sometimes he comes here."
> "He comes here at six o'clock, don't he?"
> "If he comes."
> "We know all that, bright boy," Max said. "Talk about something else. Ever go to the movies?"
> "Once in a while."
> "You ought to go to the movies more. The movies are fine for a bright boy like you."
> "What are you going to kill Ole Anderson for? What did he ever do to you?"
> "He never had a chance to do anything to us. He never even seen us."
> "And he's only going to see us once," Al said from the kitchen."
> "The Killers," in *Stories*, p. 283

Nick Adams (whom many equate with a young Hemingway and whom some consider the first fully realized example of an "apprentice" hero) appears in a number of Hemingway's short stories, but in "The Killers," Nick's worldview is greatly changed by his brush with both the casual brutality of the world and the doomed man's acquiescence to his fate. Arthur Waldhorn argues that "The Killers" "brings Nick's adolescence to a bruising close."

"A Clean, Well-Lighted Place" (1933)

Malcolm Cowley identifies the theme of "A Clean, Well-Lighted Place" with one of the disillusionments of the "inter-war generation," that is, the "disillusionment . . . with life itself." Cowley notes that the story "ends on a note of absolute nihilism that seems . . . more extreme and, in a way, more terrifying than anything written in pre-revolutionary Russia."

The story line of "A Clean, Well-Lighted Place" is simple. An elderly, deaf man sits in a café drinking brandy.

Two waiters—one young and one old—tend the café. The elderly man, who attempted suicide a week earlier, wants to spend his time in a clean, well-lit café, a desire the young waiter does not understand. The young waiter closes early, so that he can get home to his wife, sending the old man away, but the older waiter understands the old man's need. After the café is closed, the old waiter goes to a bar where he orders a coffee. We discover that he too appreciates a clean, well-lit spot, without music, where he can offset the sense of nothingness that surrounds him.

The most frequently examined term in this story as far as Hemingway studies go is *nada* (Spanish for "nothing"), which the old man uses to describe the nature of the universe. Poignantly, the old waiter replaces words in the Lord's Prayer and Hail Mary to indicate the denial of religious systems. Scholar Joseph F. Gabriel writes:

> The most dramatic representation of this nihilism is to be found in the older waiter's ironic parody of the Lord's Prayer: "Our nada who art in nada, nada be thy name." He prays; but though, on one level, his prayer is a nostalgic glance at a pattern of belief, obviously Catholicism, which once gave meaning to the whole of life, on another level, it is a denial that any system is capable of conferring order upon the chaos. And in the place of the absent God and the missing Mary, he enthrones the Nothingness which he sees all around him: "Hail nothing full of nothing, nothing is with thee."

"The Short Happy Life of Francis Macomber" (1936)

Hemingway completed "The Short Happy Life of Francis Macomber" (then titled "The Happy Ending") on April 19, 1936. Like many of Hemingway's stories, its characters and events were based on people he had met on safari in Africa in 1934. The story was first published in *Cosmopolitan* magazine in September 1936. This and "The Snows of Kilimanjaro" are arguably the two most frequently examined short stories in Hemingway's canon. One issue that has generated discussion is the "controversy over Mrs. Macomber's motives at the end of the story."

The story follows Francis Macomber, a wealthy Englishman who goes on safari to add spice to his marriage. His wife, Margot, is a woman with striking looks but no better romantic prospects than her attractive, somewhat skittish husband. At the opening of the story, Macomber has already embarrassed himself by showing fear during the hunting of a lion. Margot is disgusted by her husband's cowardice and openly involves herself with Robert Wilson, the White Hunter hired to lead the safari. Wilson is Macomber's foil. He has no fear and is comfortable in the rugged, masculine life of a hunter.

The day after the lion incident, Wilson leads Macomber and his wife on a buffalo hunt. They quickly spot three buffalo. Macomber takes the first down and the two men take the next two together. A change occurs in Macomber. He loses his fear and becomes, in Wilson's view, a man. Invigorated by his newfound courage, Macomber says he wants to try for another lion. Margot, who realizes that the change represents the end of her ability to control her husband, is unhappy about the killing of the buffalo.

They discover that the first bull is not dead and has gone into the brush. Wilson and Macomber go after it (just as they had with the lion). When the bull charges them, Macomber stands his ground, trying to make a shot through the nose. Wilson is to the side, trying to line up a shoulder shot. From her position in the car, Margot shoots her husband's 6.5 Mannlicher and hits her husband "about two inches up and a little to one side of the base of his skull" (*Stories*, p. 36).

> "You know I don't think I'd ever be afraid of anything again," Macomber said to Wilson. "Something happened in me after we first saw the buff and started after him. Like a dam bursting. It was pure excitement."
> "Cleans out your liver," said Wilson. "Damn funny things happen to people."
> Macomber's face was shining. "You know something did happen to me," he said. "I feel absolutely different."
> His wife said nothing and eyed him strangely.
> "The Short Happy Life of Francis Macomber," p. 32

Wilson clearly suspects that Margot shot him on purpose, but the ending is ambiguous. Another possible interpretation is that Margot was aiming for the charging buffalo and missed. It is this ending that has, as Thomas Strychacz notes, "made 'The Short Happy Life of Francis Macomber' the most anthologized, the most representative and . . . the most controversial short story in the Hemingway canon."

"The Snows of Kilimanjaro" (1936)

"The Snows of Kilimanjaro" is another of Hemingway's stories inspired by his first African safari. Hemingway began the story in 1935 and recognized its importance. He said that he had "put into one short story things you would use in, say, four novels if you were careful and not a spender," and claimed that it was inspired by an offer a wealthy woman had made to him to fund him in Africa. Hemingway turned down the offer, but wondered what might have happened to him if he had accepted.

Hemingway's counterpart in "The Snows of Kilimanjaro" is Harry Walden, a writer on safari in Tanzania with his wife, a wealthy woman who supports him.

"The Snows of Kilimanjaro" was made into a movie in 1952 starring Gregory Peck and Ava Gardner. It is shown on television to this day.

Harry has gangrene in his right leg from a thorn scratch he received two weeks earlier while trying to photograph a herd of waterbuck. They are waiting for the plane to pick them up, but Harry knows he is dying and he spends his last day considering his life and the choices he has made. He regrets all the stories he has not yet written. Interspersed between barbed conversations Harry has with his wife, five beautifully rendered sections represent the writing he mentally completes as he moves closer to death.

He resents his wife and blames her for her wealth, which he feels has distracted him from his writing, claiming that "each day of not writing, of comfort, of being that which he despised, dulled his ability and softened his will to work so that, finally, he did no work at all" (*Stories*, p. 59). In the end, Hemingway skillfully merges the mental life of the dying writer with the exposition of the last moments of his life: Harry wakes in the morning to the sound of the plane, whose pilot loads him onboard and, leaving Harry's wife behind, flies him over the African landscape, turning in the end toward Kilimanjaro—their destination. But Harry's rescue is only imagined. The cry of a hyena wakes Harry's wife from a dream. She looks over in horror to discover Harry's bandages unraveled, his gangrenous leg hanging off the cot, and no breath left in his lungs.

> There was no answer and she could not hear him breathing.
> Outside the tent the hyena made the same strange noise that had awakened her. But she did not hear him for the beating of her heart.
> "The Snows of Kilimanjaro," p. 77

When "The Snows of Kilimanjaro" was published in *Esquire* in 1936, it contained a passage that jabbed at F. Scott Fitzgerald, who six months earlier had published an essay about his nervous breakdown in the same magazine. Fitzgerald took offense and Hemingway changed the Fitzgerald character's name to "Julian." At issue was Fitzgerald's fascination with the very wealthy, which fit seamlessly with the theme of Hemingway's story.

Harry is a selfish and insensitive character who married a woman he did not love because she was rich. At times, he treats her cruelly, but Hemingway manages to build sympathy for the character and exposes his human vulnerability. Many critics feel, as does James R. Mellow, that "The Snows of Kilimanjaro" is "unquestionably the great masterpiece among . . . [Hemingway's] short stories."

Journalism

Hemingway began his professional writing career as a journalist. He wrote articles for five decades, beginning with his work as a reporter for the *Kansas City Star* in 1917 and continuing late into his life. He was particularly active in journalism while in Paris during the 1920s. In addition to the *Kansas City Star*, his articles covered a broad range of topics and appeared in the *Toronto Daily Star*, the *Toronto Star Weekly*, *Colliers*, the [London] *Daily Express*, *Journalism Quarterly*, *Esquire*, *Pravda*, *Sports Illustrated*, the *Transatlantic Review*, the *Mark Twain Journal*, *Life*, and other periodicals. Many of these works have been collected and posthumously published in books, such as *Hemingway, The Wild Years* (1962), *By-Line: Ernest Hemingway* (1967), *Ernest Hemingway: Cub Reporter* (1970), *Ernest Hemingway, Dateline: Toronto* (1985), and *Hemingway: The Toronto Years* (1994).

Hemingway wrote to Gertrude Stein in 1923 that he was giving up journalism, but it is clear from his continued ventures into the genre that journalism enriched his writing. Scholar Elizabeth Dewberry wrote: "Although Hemingway often complained that journalism robbed him of the juices he needed to write fiction, there is evidence that moving among journalism, creative nonfiction, and fiction stimulated all his writing." Michael Reynolds points out that "To read through Hemingway's journalism in chronological order is to read a personal history of the first half of the twentieth century as seen through the eyes of a trained, opinionated observer."

Poetry

Hemingway published twenty-five poems during his professional career, most in the 1920s during his early days as a writer. Nevertheless, Hemingway did occasionally write poems as late as the 1950s. He never planned to be a poet, nor did he aggressively pursue the genre, but he appreciated the form. Ezra Pound praised his early verse. His first book was a collection of three short stories and ten poems. In the following poem from *Three Stories and Ten Poems*, Hemingway compares his typewriter to a French precursor to the machine gun (mitrailleuse), which proved to be an ineffective weapon.

Mitrailliatrice

The mills of the gods grind slowly;
But this mill
Chatters in mechanical staccato.
Ugly short infantry of the mind,
Advancing over difficult terrain,
Make this Corona
Their mitrailleuse.

"Mitrailliatrice" was written in Chicago in 1921 and first published in the journal *Poetry* in 1923.

Book-length Nonfiction

Hemingway published two book-length works of creative nonfiction. Both were written and published in the 1930s and both dealt with subjects central to Hemingway's life.

The first was *Death in the Afternoon*, published in September 1932. *Death in the Afternoon* explained bullfighting to American audiences. Hemingway fancied himself an expert on the sport, at least among Americans. He says of the book: "It is intended as an introduction to the modern Spanish bullfight and attempts to explain that spectacle both emotionally and practically. It was written because there was no book which did this in Spanish or in English."

> A really brave fighting bull is afraid of nothing on earth and in various towns in Spain in special and barbarous exhibitions a bull has charged an elephant repeatedly; bulls have killed both lions and tigers, charging these animals as blithely as they go for the picadors. A true fighting bull fears nothing and, to me, is the finest of all animals to watch in action and repose.
> *Death in the Afternoon*, p. 109

Death in the Afternoon benefited from revisions Hemingway made at the suggestion of John Dos Passos—mainly "long passages discussing literary life, the creative writing process and Hemingway's paeans of praise for Key West—all of which he [Dos Passos] described candidly as 'unnecessary tripe.'" Despite Hemingway's changes, the books still contained much of Hemingway's personality—too much for some critics. R. L. Duffus, in his *New York Times* review, criticized Hemingway for "reminiscent emotional jag[s]" and claimed that "the famous Hemingway style is neither so clear nor so forceful in most passages of *Death in the Afternoon* as it is in his novels and short stories." Despite observations like these, *Death in the Afternoon* was generally well-received.

In 1934, after returning from his first African safari, Hemingway wrote *Green Hills of Africa*. The manuscript was serialized in *Scribners Magazine* and published as a book in October 1935. Scholar Lawrence H. Martin offers a good summary of Hemingway's goal in writing *Green Hills of Africa*:

> To tell the truth about Africa and the hunt while avoiding mistakes and melodrama of other books of the type, and thus to be the best, the most original, the most truthful of the genre, communicating personal experience in such a way as to make the armchair sportsman feel the country and the chase.

Hemingway set out to capture the landscape of Africa, which he greatly admired. For many readers, the passages dealing directly with Africa (particularly those dealing with animals) were indeed a success, though scholar Ann Putnam incisively points out that *Green Hills of Africa* can also be read as a chronicle of "the narrator's attempt to fix an image, to bring home both trophy and text, against the remorseless rush of time." The reviews were mixed—some laudatory, some harsh. Like *Death in the Afternoon, Green Hills of Africa* is rife with Hemingway's personal observations about literature. James R. Mellow notes, "As with *Death in the Afternoon*, the further Hemingway left the literary world behind him, the more the subject of literature crept into his nonfiction narratives. *Green Hills of Africa* is riddled with literary pronouncements, opinions about Rilke, Paul Valéry, Thomas Mann."

Whichever position one took on *Green Hills of Africa*, nearly everyone recognized that Hemingway's fiction was superior. In 1936 critics had two short stories to compare to Hemingway's book on Africa: "The Short Happy Life of Francis Macomber" and "The Snows of Kilimanjaro," both of which have been touted as masterpieces.

A number of books of nonfiction have appeared since Hemingway's death in 1961. The most important is *A*

Moveable Feast (1964), Hemingway's recounting of his days as an expatriate living in Paris during the 1920s. He began the book in 1957 and finished it about a year before he died.

> There is never any ending to Paris and the memory of each person who has lived in it differs from that of any other. We always returned to it no matter who we were or how it was changed or with what difficulties, or ease, it could be reached. Paris was always worth it and you received return for whatever you brought to it. But this is how Paris was in the early days when we were very poor and very happy.
> *A Moveable Feast*, p. 209

The twenty sketches that comprise *A Moveable Feast* offer insight into the life of Hemingway during the early days of his career and his relationships with other important literary figures of the time, such as Gertrude Stein, Ezra Pound, James Joyce, Ford Madox Ford, and F. Scott Fitzgerald. Because it was written in retrospect, it also gives us a view into how Hemingway's attitudes toward many of his early friends turned caustic. Frederick Busch notes that in it "we experience Hemingway's ingratitude, his viciousness to Ford Madox Ford, to F. Scott Fitzgerald, to Gertrude Stein; and when we consider his treatment of Stein, we have to recall Hemingway's defamation of homosexuals." But Busch and others are careful to point out that Hemingway's ungracious handling of his acquaintances in print does not diminish his literary contribution to modern literature.

In 1960 Hemingway wrote a 120,000-word manuscript on bullfighting. The work dealt primarily with two fighters—Antonio Ordóñez and Luis Miguel Dominguín—during the 1959 season in Spain. The work was titled

The Dangerous Summer, trimmed to 45,000 words, and published in three installments in *Life* magazine. Another edited version of the manuscript was published as a book in 1985.

Several other book-length works were published between 1999 and 2004: *Ernest Hemingway on Writing*, *Hemingway on Fishing*, *Hemingway on Hunting*, and *Hemingway on War*. The first was edited by Larry W. Phillips. The other three were pieced together from various sources by Hemingway's grandson, Sean Hemingway.

Although Hemingway is known primarily for his fiction, his nonfiction greatly contributes to the enduring legacy of one of America's best-known literary figures. To this day, Hemingway remains an icon of modern American literature, an inspiration to new authors, and a prominent personality in the history of the twentieth century.

Chronology

1899
Ernest Hemingway is born in Oak Park, Illinois, on July 21.

1917
Graduates from Oak Park and River Forest High School. Works as a reporter for the *Kansas City Star*.

1918
Travels to Italy to drive an ambulance for the Red Cross.

July 8, wounded in Fossalta. While recuperating at a hospital in Milan, he meets and falls in love with Agnes von Kurowsky.

1919
Returns to the United States. Shortly thereafter, Agnes ends their relationship.

1921
Marries Elizabeth Hadley Richardson on September 3, and they move to Paris.

1923
The Hemingways travel to Canada to have their first child on North American soil.

Hemingway's first book, *Three Stories and Ten Poems,* is published.

Hadley gives birth to John Hadley Nicanor ("Bumby") in Toronto, Canada, on October 10.

1924
January 19, the Hemingways return to Paris.

1925

In Our Time published.

1926

The Torrents of Spring published by Charles Scribners Sons (which becomes Hemingway's publisher for the rest of his career).

The Sun Also Rises published.

1927

Hemingway divorces his first wife, Hadley.

Hemingway marries Pauline Pfeiffer on May 10.

Men Without Women published.

1928

Hemingway and Pauline move to Key West, Florida.

June 28, Pauline gives birth to Patrick Hemingway in Kansas City, Missouri.

December 6, Hemingway's father commits suicide.

1929

Hemingway and Pauline visit Paris.

A Farewell to Arms published.

1930

Hemingway and Pauline return to Key West.

Hemingway shatters his arm in an automobile accident in Billings, Montana.

1931

Hemingway and Pauline buy the house at 907 Whitehead Street in Key West with money from Pauline's Uncle Gus.

November 12, Pauline gives birth to Gregory Hancock Hemingway in Kansas City, Missouri.

1932

Death in the Afternoon published.

1933
Winner Take Nothing published.
Hemingway and Pauline begin African safari.
Hemingway buys boat, which he christens the *Pilar*.

1935
Green Hills of Africa published.

1936
In Key West, Hemingway meets Martha Gellhorn at Sloppy Joe's Bar.

1937
Hemingway travels to Spain to cover the Spanish Civil War as a war correspondent for the North American News Alliance (NANA).

In Madrid, Hemingway continues relationship with Martha, and works with Joris Ivens on documentary, *The Spanish Earth*. Hemingway writes the narration and provides the voiceover for the film (replacing Orson Welles).

To Have and Have Not published.

1939
Narration of *The Spanish Earth* film published in book form by J. B. Savage Company.

The Fifth Column and the First Forty-nine Stories published.

In December, Hemingway leaves his home in Key West and takes up permanent residence in Cuba.

1940
Hemingway and Pauline divorce on November 4.

Hemingway and Martha marry on November 21.

Hemingway's play, *The Fifth Column*, opens on March 7 in New York. *The Fifth Column* published.

For Whom the Bell Tolls published.

1941
Hemingway travels with Martha to China to cover the Sino-Japanese War.

1942
Hemingway establishes an amateur spy network in Cuba.
Hemingway arms the *Pilar* and uses it to patrol the waters around Cuba, looking for German submarines.

1944
Hemingway and Martha travel to London separately to cover the war.
Hemingway meets Mary Welsh and the two begin a relationship.
Hemingway involved in another automobile accident and gets a concussion. Begins to have severe headaches.
In August, Hemingway involved in another automobile accident, which results in another concussion. He develops double vision.
Hemingway organizes a band of partisans and enters Paris. In October, he faces an Army hearing for violating the Geneva Convention and overstepping his bounds as a journalist. He lies his way out of trouble.

1945
Hemingway and Martha begin divorce proceedings in London.
Hemingway returns to Cuba. Mary follows.
Hemingway and Martha divorce on December 21.

1946
Hemingway and Mary marry on March 14.

1947
Hemingway is awarded the Bronze Star.

1948
Hemingway begins work on *Islands in the Stream.*

1950
Across the River and Into the Trees published.

Hemingway involved in boating accident and damages his head again.

1951
Hemingway's mother dies on June 28.

Pauline dies on October 1.

1952
The Old Man and the Sea published.

1953
Hemingway awarded the Pulitzer Prize for *The Old Man and the Sea.*

1954
Hemingway and Mary involved in two plane crashes, injuring his head for the fourth time.

Hemingway awarded the Nobel Prize.

1960
Hemingway's health is in decline and he is suffering from severe depression. He travels to Spain, where friends notice the change in him. Mary retrieves him.

November, admitted to the Mayo Clinic.

1961
The Snows of Kilimanjaro and Other Stories is published.

Hemingway twice attempts suicide. He is readmitted to the Mayo Clinic in April, where he receives electroshock treatments. He is discharged at the end of June and commits suicide on the morning of July 2.

1964
A Moveable Feast published.

1970
Islands in the Stream published.

1972
The Nick Adams Stories published.

1979
Ernest Hemingway: Complete Poems published by University of Nebraska Press.

1985
The Dangerous Summer published.

1986
The Garden of Eden published.

1987
The Complete Short Stories of Ernest Hemingway published.

1999
True at First Light published.

List of Works

Novels

The Torrents of Spring. New York: Scribner, 1926.
The Sun Also Rises. New York: Scribner, 1926.
A Farewell to Arms. New York: Scribner, 1929.
To Have and Have Not. New York: Scribner, 1937.
For Whom the Bell Tolls. New York: Scribner, 1940.
Across the River and Into the Trees. New York: Scribner, 1950.
The Old Man and the Sea. New York: Scribner, 1952.
Islands in the Stream. New York: Scribner, 1970.
The Garden of Eden. New York: Scribner, 1986.
True at First Light. New York: Scribner, 1999.

Short Story Collections

Three Stories and Ten Poems. Paris: Contact, 1923.
In Our Time. Paris: Three Mountain Press, 1924.
In Our Time. New York: Boni & Liveright, 1925.
Men Without Women. New York: Scribner, 1927.
Winner Take Nothing. New York: Scribner, 1933.
The Fifth Column and the First Forty-nine Stories. New York: Scribner, 1938.
The Nick Adams Stories. New York: Scribner, 1972.
The Complete Short Stories of Ernest Hemingway: The Finca Vigía Edition. New York: Scribner, 1987.
The Snows of Kilimanjaro and Other Stories. New York: Scribner, 1995.
The Collected Stories. Ed. James Fenton. New York: Everyman Publishers, 1995.

Nonfiction

Death in the Afternoon. New York: Scribner, 1932.
Green Hills of Africa. New York: Scribner, 1935.
A Moveable Feast. New York: Scribner, 1964.
The Dangerous Summer. New York: Scribner, 1985.

Plays

Today is Friday. Published in *Men Without Women*. New York: Scribner, 1926.
The Fifth Column and the First Forty-nine Stories. New York: Scribner, 1938.

Screenplays

Spain in Flames (Hemingway helped write commentary). Compilation film of the Spanish Civil War. Edited by Helen van Dongen. 1937.

The Spanish Earth (with John Dos Passos, Prudencio de Pereda, Lillian Hellman, Joris Ivens, and Archibald Macleish). Documentary. Dir. Joris Ivens. Prod. Contemporary Historians. 1937.

Collections of Poetry

Three Stories and Ten Poems: Paris. Contact, 1923.

Ernest Hemingway: 88 Poems. New York: Harcourt Brace Jovanovich, 1979.

Ernest Hemingway: Complete Poems. Lincoln: University of Nebraska Press, 1979.

Ernest Hemingway: Complete Poems. Rev. ed. Ed. Nicholas Gerogiannis. Lincoln: University of Nebraska Press, 1992.

Collections of Essays and Articles

Hemingway, The Wild Years. Ed. Gene Hanrahan. New York: Dell, 1962.

By-Line: Ernest Hemingway: Selected Articles and Dispatches of Four Decades. Ed. William White. New York: Scribner, 1967.

Ernest Hemingway: Cub Reporter. Ed. Matthew Bruccoli. New York: University of Pittsburgh Press, 1970.

Ernest Hemingway, Dateline: Toronto. Ed. William White. New York: Scribner, 1985.

Hemingway: The Toronto Years. Ed. William Burrill. Canada: Doubleday, 1994.

Other Writings and Collections

The Hemingway Reader. Ed. Charles Poore. New York: Scribner, 1953.

Ernest Hemingway, Selected Letters, 1917–1961. Ed. Carlos Baker. New York: Scribner, 1981.

Ernest Hemingway on Writing. Ed. Larry W. Phillips. New York: Scribner, 1999.

Hemingway on Fishing. Ed. Sean Hemingway. New York: Lyons Press, 2000.

Hemingway on Hunting. Ed. Sean Hemingway. New York: Lyons Press, 2001.

Hemingway on War. Ed. Sean Hemingway. New York: Scribner, 2004.

Filmography

A Farewell to Arms. Dir. Frank Borzage. 1932.

The Spanish Earth. (Documentary) Dir. Joris Ivens. 1937.

For Whom the Bell Tolls. Dir. Sam Wood. 1943.

To Have and Have Not. Dir. Howard Hawks. 1944.

The Killers. Dir. Richard Siodmak. 1946.

The Macomber Affair. Dir. Zoltan Korda. 1947.

Under My Skin. Dir. Jean Negulesco. 1950.

The Breaking Point. Dir. Michael Curtiz. 1950.

The Snows of Kilimanjaro. Dir. Henry King. 1952.

The Sun Also Rises. Dir. Henry King. 1957.

A Farewell to Arms. Dir. Charles Vidor. 1957.

Ubiitsy. Dir. Marika Beiku, Aleksandr Gordon, and Andrei Tarkovsky. 1958.

The Old Man and the Sea. Dir. by John Sturges. 1958.

The Gun Runners. Dir. Don Siegel. Screenplay by Daniel Mainwaring and Paul Monash. 1958.

Adeus às Armas. (TV). Series produced in Brazil, based on *A Farewell to Arms* by Ernest Hemingway. 1961.

Ernest Hemingway's Adventures as a Young Man. Dir. Martin Ritt. 1962.

The Killers. Dir. Don Siegel. 1964.

For Whom the Bell Tolls. (TV). Dir. Rex Tucker. 1965.

Notes

Part I: The Life of Ernest Hemingway
Chapter 1

p. 9, Burgess, Anthony, *Ernest Hemingway* (New York: Thames and Hudson, 1978), p. 9.

p. 9, Biographer Kenneth S. Lynn claims that Grace's cross-dressing of Ernest resulted in sexual confusion and influenced his writing.

p. 9, "I don't know Buffalo Bill." Baker, Carlos, *Ernest Hemingway: A Life Story* (New York: Collier Books, 1969).

p. 10, Baker, *Ernest Hemingway*: *A Life Story*, p. 5.

p. 10, Baker, *Ernest Hemingway*: *A Life Story*, p. 12.

p. 10, Baker, *Ernest Hemingway*: *A Life Story*, p. 27.

p. 11, Burgess, *Ernest Hemingway*, p. 15.

p. 12, This list compiled from Carlos Baker's *Ernest Hemingway*: *A Life Story* (p. 34) and Michael Reynolds, "A Brief Biography" (p. 22).

p. 13, Qtd. Reynolds, "1899–1961," p. 22.

p. 15, Baker, *Ernest Hemingway*: *A Life Story*, p. 44.

p. 15, Meyers, *Hemingway*: *A Biography*, p. 30.

p. 15, Meyers, *Hemingway*: *A Biography*, p. 32.

p. 15, Meyers, *Hemingway*: *A Biography*, p. 36.

p. 15, Meyers, *Hemingway*: *A Biography*, p. 35.

p. 17, Waldhorn, *A Reader's Guide to Ernest Hemingway* (New York: Farrar, Straus and Giroux, 1972), p. 8.

p. 17, Waldhorn, *A Reader's Guide to Ernest Hemingway* (1972), p. 8.

p. 17, Burgess, *Ernest Hemingway*, p. 24.

p. 18, Qtd. Baker, *Ernest Hemingway: A Life Story*, p. 84.

p. 19, Sandison, David. *Ernest Hemingway: An Illustrated Biography* (Chicago: Chicago Review, 1999).

p. 19, Sandison, *Ernest Hemingway: An Illustrated Biography*, p. 62.

p. 22, *New York Times Book Review* (Oct. 18, 1925), p. 8.

p. 23, Cf. "Books and Authors," *New York Times Book Review* (Apr. 25, 1926), p. 18.

p. 23, *New York Times Book Review* (June 13, 1926), p. 8.

p. 24, Qtd. Sandison, *Ernest Hemingway: An Illustrated Biography*, p. 88.

p. 24, Baker, *Ernest Hemingway: A Life Story*, p. 178.

p. 25, Sandison, *Ernest Hemingway: An Illustrated Biography*, p. 99.

p. 26, Baker, *Ernest Hemingway: A Life Story*, p. 251.

p. 26, Qtd. Baker, *Ernest Hemingway: A Life Story*, p. 268.

p. 26, Carlos Baker in his biography on Hemingway points out that Arnold Gingrich was of the opinion that F. Scott Fitzgerald's depression would "bring out the bully" in Hemingway. (Baker, *Ernest Hemingway: A Life Story*, p. 282).

p. 28, Baker, *Ernest Hemingway: A Life Story*, p. 274.

p. 28, Poore, C. G. "Ernest Hemingway's Story of His African Safari." *New York Times Book Review* (Oct. 27, 1935), p. 3.

p. 28, Poore, *New York Times Book Review* (Oct. 27, 1935), p. BR3.

p. 28, Baker, *Ernest Hemingway: A Life Story*, p. 261.

p. 28, Qtd. Baker, *Ernest Hemingway: A Life Story*, p. 262.

p. 29, Baker, *Ernest Hemingway: A Life Story*, p. 277. Kashkeen's essay was published and read by Hemingway prior to the publication of *Green Hills of Africa*.

p. 29, Qtd. Mellow, James R. *Hemingway: A Life Without Consequences* (New York: Houghton Mifflin, 1992), p. 479.

p. 30, Baker, *Ernest Hemingway: A Life Story*, p. 321.
Wagner-Martin, Linda, ed. *A Historical Guide to Ernest Hemingway* (New York: Oxford University Press, 2000), p. 34.

p. 31, Sandison, *Ernest Hemingway: An Illustrated Biography*, p. 118.

p. 32, Baker, *Ernest Hemingway: A Life Story*, p. 375.

p. 33, Qtd. Baker, *Ernest Hemingway: A Life Story*, p. 392–393.

p. 33, Baker, *Ernest Hemingway: A Life Story*, p. 410.

p. 34, Baker, *Ernest Hemingway: A Life Story*, p. 445.

p. 35, Cf. O'Hara, John. "The Author's Name is Hemingway." *New York Times* (Sep. 10, 1950).

p. 35, Baker, *Ernest Hemingway: A Life Story*, p. 489.

p. 35, Qtd. Baker, *Ernest Hemingway: A Life Story*, pp. 503–504.

p. 35, *See* "Clean and Straight."

p. 37, Baker, *Ernest Hemingway: A Life Story*, p. 522.

p. 37, Qtd. Baker, *Ernest Hemingway: A Life Story*, p. 528.

p. 37, Baker, *Ernest Hemingway: A Life Story*, p. 552.

Chapter 2

p. 39, Hatcher, Harlan. "The Second Lost Generation." *The English Journal* 25.8 (October 1936, pp. 621–631), p. 621.

p. 40, Some date the beginning of the period as early as 1900 and others as late as 1930.

p. 40, This list is culled from the entry on "Modern" in C. Hugh Holman and William Harmon's *A Handbook to Literature,* 5th ed.

p. 41, Qtd. Burgess, *Ernest Hemingway*, p. 109.

Part II: The Writing of Ernest Hemingway
Introduction

p. 51, Young, Philip. *Ernest Hemingway* (Minneapolis: University of Minnesota Press, 1959), p. 17.

p. 52, *See* Waldhorn, *A Reader's Guide to Ernest Hemingway* (1972), p. 23.

p. 52, Waldhorn bases his argument on the earlier work of Philip Young and Earl Rovit. Cf. Waldhorn's *A Reader's Guide to Ernest Hemingway* (1972), p. 23.

p. 52, Waldhorn, *A Reader's Guide to Ernest Hemingway* (1972), pp. 24–25.

p. 52, Waldhorn, *A Reader's Guide to Ernest Hemingway* (1972), p. 23.

Chapter 1

p. 55, Reynolds, Michael. *Ernest Hemingway: Vol. 2, Literary Masters* (Farmington Hills, MI: Gale Group, 2000), p. 4–5.

p. 55, Mellow, *Hemingway*, p. 303.

p. 55, Wagner-Martin, Linda, ed. *Ernest Hemingway's* The Sun Also Rises: *A Casebook* (New York: Oxford University Press, 2002), p. 3.

p. 56, Hemingway, Leicester. *My Brother, Ernest Hemingway* (Sarasota, FL: Pineapple Press, 1996), p. 100.

p. 56, Wagner-Martin, Linda, ed. *New Essays on* The Sun Also Rises (New York: Cambridge University Press, 1987), p. 1.

p. 58, Rudat, Wolfgang E. H. "Anti-Semitism in *The Sun Also Rises*: Traumas, Jealousies, and the Genesis of Cohn." *Hemingway: Up in Michigan Perspectives*. Eds. Frederic J. Svoboda and Joseph J. Waldmeir. (East Lansing: Michigan State University Press, 1995, pp. 137–147), p. 138.

p. 58, *See* Wolfgang E. H. Rudat, "Anti-Semitism in *The Sun Also Rises*: Traumas, Jealousies, and the Genesis of Cohn," p. 138.

p. 59, Nagel, James. "Narrational Values and Robert Cohn in *The Sun Also Rises. Hemingway, Up in Michigan Perspectives*. Eds. Frederic J. Svoboda and Joseph J. Waldmeir. (East Lansing: Michigan State University Press, 1995, pp. 129–136), p. 131.

p. 60, Martin, Wendy. “Brett Ashley as New Woman.” *New Essays on* The Sun Also Rises. Ed. Linda Wagner-Martin. (New York: Cambridge University Press, 1987, pp. 65–82), p. 69.

p. 60, Sokoloff, Alice Hunt, *Hadley: The First Mrs. Hemingway* (New York: Dodd, 1973), p. 81.

p. 61, Donaldson, Scott, ed. *The Cambridge Companion to Ernest Hemingway* (New York: Cambridge University Press, 1996), p. 89.

p. 61, Hemingway characterizes the code hero as “a man who lives correctly, following the ideals of honor, courage and endurance in a world that is sometimes chaotic, often stressful, and always painful.”

p. 61, Young, *Ernest Hemingway*, p. 14.

p. 63, Waldhorn, *A Reader's Guide to Ernest Hemingway* (1972), p. 101.

p. 65, Qtd. Bruccoli, Matthew J. *Classes on Ernest Hemingway* (Columbia: University of South Carolina, 2002), p. 37.

p. 65, Qtd. Donaldson, Scott. *Hemingway vs. Fitzgerald: The Rise and Fall of a Literary Friendship*. (New York: Overlook Press, 1999), p. 96.

p. 65, Reynolds, Michael. “Recovering the Historical Context.” *New Essays on* The Sun Also Rises. Ed. Linda Wagner-Martin. (New York: Cambridge University Press, 1987, 43–64), p. 53.

p. 80, Waldhorn, *A Reader's Guide to Ernest Hemingway* (1972), p. 95.

p. 90, Baker, *Ernest Hemingway: A Life Story*, p. 359.

p. 90, Carlos Baker, *Ernest Hemingway: A Life Story*, p. 383.

p. 90, Donaldson, Scott. “Hemingway's Morality of Compensation.” *Ernest Hemingway's* The Sun Also Rises*: A Casebook*. Ed. Linda Wagner-Martin. (New York: Oxford University Press, 2002, 81–98), p. 82.

p. 92, Halliday, E. M., “Hemingway's Ambiguity: Symbolism and Irony” (*American Literature* 28, 1956, pp. 1–22), p. 7.

Chapter 2

p. 93, Baker, *Ernest Hemingway: A Life Story*, p. 339.

p. 93, Later it was a planned trilogy. Cf. David Sandison, *Ernest Hemingway: Illustrated Biography*, p. 136.

p. 93, Baker, *Ernest Hemingway: A Life Story*, p. 492.

p. 93, Hemingway, Leicester. *My Brother, Ernest Hemingway*, p. 273.

p. 95, Reynolds, Michael. “Ernest Hemingway 1899–1961: A Brief Biography.” *A Historical Guide to Ernest Hemingway*. Ed. Linda Wagner-Martin. (New York: Oxford University Press, 2000, 15–50), p. 45.

p. 100, *The Old Man and the Sea* has no chapter or section divisions. The divisions here are used for convenience.

p. 101, Melito, Ignatius M., "The Literary Myth-Makers" (*The English Journal* 53, 1964, pp. 165–169), p. 168.

p. 101, Halliday, "Hemingway's Ambiguity: Symbolism and Irony," p. 2.

p. 101, Valenti, Patricia Dunlavy. *Understanding* The Old Man and the Sea (Westport, CT: Greenwood, 2002), p. 12.

p. 102, Waldhorn, *A Reader's Guide to Ernest Hemingway* (New York: Syracuse UP, 2002), p. 192.

p. 102, Waldhorn, *A Reader's Guide to Ernest Hemingway* (2002), p. 193.

Chapter 3

p. 103, Cf. Baker, *Ernest Hemingway: A Life Story*, p. 199.

p. 105, Oldsey, Bernard. "The Sense of an Ending." *Critical Essays on Ernest Hemingway's* A Farewell to Arms. Ed. George Monteiro. (New York: G.K. Hall, 1994, pp. 47–64), p. 47.

p. 107, Waldhorn, *A Reader's Guide to Ernest Hemingway* (1972), p. 129.

p. 107, Qtd. Meyers, *Hemingway: A Biography*, p. 296.

p. 107, Qtd. Meyers, *Hemingway: A Biography*, p. 296.

p. 108, Adams, J. Donald. "The New Novel by Hemingway." *New York Times Book Review* (Oct. 20, 1940), p. 93.

p. 109, p. 113, Messent, Peter. *Modern Novelists: Ernest Hemingway* (New York: St. Martin's Press, 1992), pp. 74–75.

p. 110, Adams, J. Donald. "Speaking of Books." *New York Times Book Review* (Sep. 24, 1950), p. 2.

p. 110, Adams, *New York Times Book Review* (Sep. 24, 1950), p. 2.

p. 110, O'Hara, John. "The Author's Name is Hemingway." (*New York Times*, Sep. 10, 1950), p. 200.

p. 111, Burwell, Rose Marie. *The Postwar Years and the Posthumous Novels*. (New York: Cambridge University Press, 1996), p. 1.

p. 112, Marita is actually a bisexual, attracted to both Catherine and David, but she is introduced as a lesbian involved in a relationship with another woman (Nina).

p. 113, Miller, Linda Patterson. "In Love with Papa." *Hemingway and Women: Female Critics and the Female Voice*. Eds. Lawrence R. Broer and Gloria Holland. (Tuscaloosa: Uneversity of Alabama Press, 2004, 3–23), p. 6.

p. 113, Baker, *Ernest Hemingway: A Life Story*, p. 526.

p. 114, Qtd. Goldberg, Carey. "Hemingway Gets a Kick in a Kickoff." (*New York Times*, Apr. 14, 1999, E1, 4), p. B4.

Chapter 4

p. 116, García Márquez, Gabriel. "Gabriel García Márquez Meets Ernest Hemingway." (*New York Times Book Review*, July 26, 1981, pp. 1, 16–17), p. 16.

p. 116, Smith, Paul, ed. *New Essays on Hemingway's Short Fiction* (New York: Cambridge University Press, 1998), p. 1.

p. 116, McAlmon, Robert. *Being Geniuses Together* (London: Secker & Warburg, 1938), p. 159.

p. 116, Charles M. Oliver in *Ernest Hemingway A to Z*. (New York: Facts On File, 1999) says the rail junction is "probably . . . about 9 miles northwest of Zaragoza, where the main line Between Barcelona and Madrid meets the line that runs on to the northwest" (p. 152).

p. 117, Reynolds, "Ernest Hemingway 1899–1961: A Brief Biography," p. 30.

p. 118, Hemingway, Ernest. "The Art of the Short Story." *Ernest Hemingway: A Study of the Short Fiction.*" Ed. Joseph M. Flora. (Boston: Twayne, 1989, pp. 129–44), pp. 139–140.

p. 118, We know from the mood and from Hemingway's comments that the story takes place in Chicago, but Chicago is never explicitly mentioned.

p. 119, The precise number of stories that feature Nick Adams is debatable. As Oliver notes, Nick Adams is "the named protagonist in 12 short stories and one of the interchapters of *In Our Time,*" but he is also "generally considered to be the protagonist in three other stories in which he is not named," and is featured in eight other "fragments of short stories or novels." (*See* Oliver, *Ernest Hemingway A to Z*, p. 3.)

p. 119, Waldhorn, *A Reader's Guide to Ernest Hemingway* (2002), p. 61.

p. 119, Cowley, Malcolm. "The Generation That Wasn't Lost." (*College English* 5, 1944, pp. 233—239), p. 237.

p. 120, Gabriel, Joseph F. "The Logic of Confusion in Hemingway's 'A Clean Well-Lighted Place.'" (*College English* 22, 1961, pp. 539—546), p. 541.

p. 121, *See* Paul Smith's thorough review of Hemingway's short fiction in *A Reader's Guide to the Short Stories of Ernest Hemingway*, p. 327.

p. 122, Strychacz, Thomas. *Hemingway's Theaters of Masculinity* (Baton Rouge: Louisiana State University Press, 2003), p. 15.

p. 122, Qtd. Mellow, James R. *Hemingway: A Life Without Consequences* (New York: Houghton Mifflin, 1992), p. 449.

p. 122, Cf. Mellow, *Hemingway: A Life Without Consequences*, p. 448.

p. 125, Mellow, *Hemingway: A Life Without Consequences*, p. 449.

p. 125, Dewberry, Elizabeth. "Hemingway's Journalism and the Realist Dilemma." *The Cambridge Companion to Ernest Hemingway.* Ed. Scott Donaldson. (New York: Cambridge University Press, 1996, pp. 16-35), p. 16.

p. 126, Reynolds, *Ernest Hemingway: Vol. 2, Literary Masters,* p. 89.

p. 127, Hemingway, *Death in the Afternoon,* p. 515.

p. 127, Sandison, *Ernest Hemingway: An Illustrated Biography*, p. 100.

p. 127, Duffus, R. L. "Hemingway Now Writes of Bull-Fighting as an Art." *New York Times Book Review* (Sept. 25, 1932), p. 5.

p. 128, Martin, Lawrence H. "Hemingway's Constructed Africa: *Green Hills of Africa* and the Conventions of Colonial Sporting Books." *Hemingway and the Natural World.* Ed. Robert E. Fleming (Moscow: University of Idaho Press, 1999, pp. 87–97), p. 88.

p. 128, Putnam, Ann. "Memory, Grief, and the Terrain of Desire: Hemingway's *Green Hills of Africa.*" *Hemingway and the Natural World.* Ed. Robert E. Fleming. (Moscow: University of Idaho Press, 1999, pp. 99–110), p. 99.

p. 128, Mellow, *Hemingway: A Life Without Consequences,* p. 436.

p. 128, p. 133, Cf. Reynolds, *Ernest Hemingway: Vol. 2, Literary Masters,* pp. 120–121.

p. 129, A. E. Hotchner cut the original 120,000-word draft down to 65,000 words, from which *Life* magazine pulled its excerpts. In 1985 the work was published as a book by Scribner's after Michael Pietsch reedited the manuscript.

Further Information

Further Reading

Bloom, Harold, ed. *Ernest Hemingway: Modern Critical Views*. New York: Roundhouse, 1991.

Oliver, Charles M., and Charles M. Robert. *Ernest Hemingway A to Z*. New York: Facts on File, 1999.

Palin, Michael. *Michael Palin's Hemingway Adventure*. New York: St. Martin's, 2001.

Pingelton, Timothy J. *A Student's Guide to Ernest Hemingway*. Berkeley Heights, NJ: Enslow Publishers, 2005.

Waldorn, Arthur. *A Reader's Guide to Ernest Hemingway*. Syracuse: Syracuse University Press, 2002.

Web Sites

The Hemingway Resource Center
http://www.lostgeneration.com

Hemingway Society
http://hemingwaysociety.org

The John F. Kennedy Presidential Library: The Ernest Hemingway Collection
http://www.jfklibrary.org/Historical+Resources/Hemingway+Archive

New York Times Featured Author Site
http://www.nytimes.com/books/99/07/11/specials/hemingway-main.html

Bibliography

Adams, J. Donald. "Speaking of Books." *New York Times Book Review* (Sep. 24, 1950): 2.

———. "The New Novel by Hemingway." *New York Times* (Oct. 20, 1940): 93.

Baker, Carlos. *Ernest Hemingway: A Life Story*. New York: Collier, 1969.

Bruccoli, Matthew J. *Classes on Ernest Hemingway*. Columbia: University of South Carolina, 2002.

Burgess, Anthony. *Ernest Hemingway*. New York: Thames and Hudson, 1978.

Burwell, Rose Marie. *The Postwar Years and the Posthumous Novels*. New York: Cambridge University Press, 1996.

"Clean and Straight." Review of *The Old Man and the Sea. Time Magazine Archive. Time Magazine*, Sep. 8, 1952: http://www.time.com

Cowley, Malcolm. "The Generation That Wasn't Lost," *College English* 5 (1944): 233–239.

DeFazio III, Albert J. *Literary Masterpieces:* The Sun Also Rises. Vol. 2, *Gale Study Guides to Great Literature*. Detroit: Gale Group, 2000.

Dewberry, Elizabeth. "Hemingway's Journalism and the Realist Dilemma." *The Cambridge Companion to*

Ernest Hemingway. Ed. Scott Donaldson. New York: Cambridge University Press, 1996: 16–35.

Donaldson, Scott. "Hemingway's Morality of Compensation." *Ernest Hemingway's* The Sun Also Rises*: A Casebook*. Ed. Linda Wagner-Martin. New York: Oxford University Press, 2002: 81–98.

———. *Hemingway vs. Fitzgerald: The Rise and Fall of a Literary Friendship*. New York: Overlook Press, 1999.

———, ed. *The Cambridge Companion to Ernest Hemingway*. New York: Cambridge University Press, 1996.

Duffus, R. L. "Hemingway Now Writes of Bull-Fighting as an Art." *New York Times Book Review* (Sept. 25, 1932): 5, 17.

Gabriel, Joseph F. "The Logic of Confusion in Hemingway's 'A Clean Well-Lighted Place,'" *College English* 22 (1961): 539–546.

García Márquez, Gabriel. "Gabriel García Márquez Meets Ernest Hemingway." *New York Times Book Review* (July 26, 1981): 1, 16–17.

Goldberg, Carey. "Hemingway Gets a Kick in a Kickoff." *New York Times* (Apr. 14, 1999): E1, 4.

Halliday, E. M. "Hemingway's Ambiguity: Symbolism and Irony." *American Literature* 28 (1956): 1–22.

Hatcher, Harlan. "The Second Lost Generation." *The English Journal* 25 (1936): 621–631.

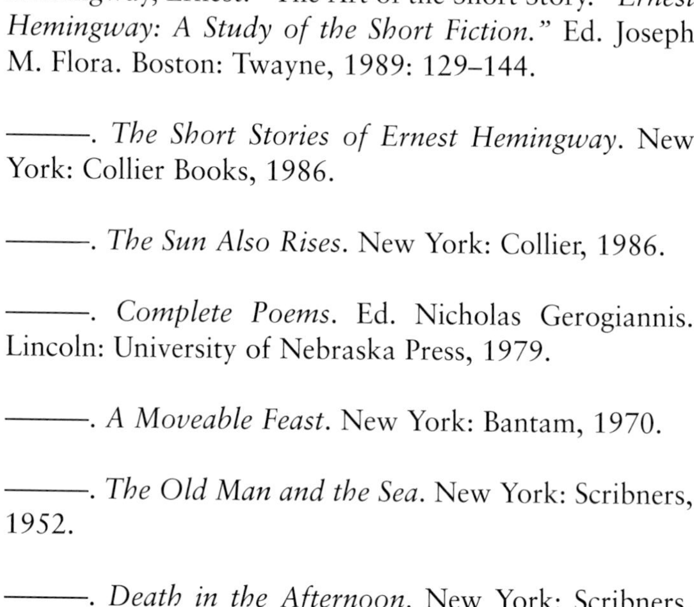

Hemingway, Ernest. “The Art of the Short Story.” *Ernest Hemingway: A Study of the Short Fiction.”* Ed. Joseph M. Flora. Boston: Twayne, 1989: 129–144.

———. *The Short Stories of Ernest Hemingway*. New York: Collier Books, 1986.

———. *The Sun Also Rises*. New York: Collier, 1986.

———. *Complete Poems*. Ed. Nicholas Gerogiannis. Lincoln: University of Nebraska Press, 1979.

———. *A Moveable Feast*. New York: Bantam, 1970.

———. *The Old Man and the Sea*. New York: Scribners, 1952.

———. *Death in the Afternoon*. New York: Scribners, 1932.

Hemingway, Leicester. *My Brother, Ernest Hemingway*. Sarasota, FL: Pineapple Press, 1996.

Holman, C. Hugh, and William Harmon. *A Handbook to Literature*, 5th ed. New York: Macmillan, 1986.

Martin, Lawrence H. “Hemingway’s Constructed Africa: *Green Hills of Africa* and the Conventions of Colonial Sporting Books.” *Hemingway and the Natural World*. Ed. Robert E. Fleming. Moscow: University of Idaho Press, 1999: 87–97.

Martin, Wendy. “Brett Ashley as New Woman.” *New Essays on* The Sun Also Rises. Ed. Linda Wagner Martin. New York: Cambridge University Press, 1987: 65–82.

McAlmon, Robert. *Being Geniuses Together*. London: Secker & Warburg, 1938.

Melito, Ignatius M. "The Literary Myth-Makers." *The English Journal* 53.3 (March 1964): 165–169.

Mellow, James R. *Hemingway: A Life Without Consequences*. New York: Houghton Mifflin, 1992.

Messent, Peter. *Modern Novelists: Ernest Hemingway*. New York: St. Martin's Press, 1992.

Meyers, Jeffrey. *Hemingway: A Biography*. New York: Da Capo, 1999.

"Mr. Hemingway Writes Some High-Spirited Nonsense." Review of *The Torrents of Spring*, *New York Times* (June 13, 1926): BR8.

Nagel, James. "Narrational Values and Robert Cohn in *The Sun Also Rises*." *Hemingway: Up in Michigan Perspectives*. Eds. Frederic J. Svoboda and Joseph J. Waldmeir. East Lansing: Michigan State University Press, 1995: 129–136.

O'Hara, John. "The Author's Name is Hemingway." *New York Times*. (Sep. 10, 1950): 200.

Oldsey, Bernard. "The Sense of and Ending." *Critical Essays on Ernest Hemingway's* A Farewell to Arms. Ed. George Monteiro. New York: G. K. Hall, 1994.

Oliver, Charles M. *Ernest Hemingway A to Z*. New York: Facts On File, 1999.

Poore, C. G. "Ernest Hemingway's Story of His African Safari." *New York Times* (Oct. 27, 1935): BR3.

———. "Preludes to a Mood." Review of *In Our Time. New York Times* (Oct. 18, 1925): BR8.

Putnam, Ann. "Memory, Grief, and the Terrain of Desire: Hemingway's *Green Hills of Africa.*" *Hemingway and the Natural World.* Moscow, Idaho: University of Idaho Press, 1999: 99–110.

Reynolds, Michael. *Ernest Hemingway: Literary Masters,* Vol. 2. Farmington Hills, MI: Gale Group, 2000.

———. "Recovering the Historical Context." *New Essays on* The Sun Also Rises. Ed. Linda Wagner-Martin. New York: Cambridge University Press, 1987: 43–64.

———. "Ernest Hemingway 1899–1961: A Brief Biography." *A Historical Guide to Ernest Hemingway.* Ed. Linda Wagner-Martin. New York: Oxford University Press, 2000: 15–50.
Rudat, Wolfgang E. H. "Anti-Semitism in *The Sun Also Rises:* Traumas, Jealousies, and the Genesis of Cohn."

Hemingway: Up in Michigan Perspectives. Eds. Frederic J. Svoboda and Joseph J. Waldmeir. East Lansing: Michigan State University Press, 1995: 137–147.

Sandison, David. *Ernest Hemingway: An Illustrated Biography.* Chicago: Chicago Review, 1999.

Smith, Paul, ed. *New Essays on Hemingway's Short Fiction.* New York: Cambridge University Press, 1998.

Sokoloff, Alice Hunt. *Hadley: The First Mrs. Hemingway.* New York: Dodd, 1973.

Strychacz, Thomas. *Hemingway's Theaters of Masculinity.*

Baton Rouge: Louisiana State University Press, 2003.

Valenti, Patricia Dunlavy. *Understanding* The Old Man and the Sea. Westport, CT: Greenwood, 2002.

Wagner-Martin, Linda, ed. *Ernest Hemingway's* The Sun Also Rises*: A Casebook*. New York: Oxford University Press, 2002.

———, ed. *A Historical Guide to Ernest Hemingway.* New York: Oxford University Press, 2000.

———, ed. *New Essays on* The Sun Also Rises. New York: Cambridge University Press, 1987.

Waldhorn, Arthur. *A Reader's Guide to Ernest Hemingway.* New York: Syracuse University Press, 2002.

Index

Page numbers in **boldface** are illustrations, tables, and charts. Proper names of fictional characters are shown by (C).

About the Author

Kevin A. Boon is an assistant professor at Pennsylvania State University and English Program Coordinator for the Mont Alto campus. He teaches film, writing, and literature, and is the author and editor of a number of books on Kurt Vonnegut, Virginia Woolf, and other writers. He is also an award-winning poet and fiction writer, a skilled composer and musician, and a produced playwright. His most recent book for Marshall Cavendish Benchmark was *F. Scott Fitzgerald:* The Great Gatsby, in this series.